P9-DDI-200

Loving Yourself as
Your Neighbor

Loving Yourself as Your Neighbor

A Recovery Guide for Christians Escaping Burnout and Codependency

CARMEN RENEE BERRY &

MARK LLOYD TAYLOR

1817

HARPER & ROW, PUBLISHERS, SAN FRANCISCO
New York, Grand Rapids, Philadelphia, St. Louis
London, Singapore, Sydney, Tokyo, Toronto

LOVING YOURSELF AS YOUR NEIGHBOR: *A Recovery Guide for Christians Escaping Burnout and Codependency*. Copyright © 1990 by Carmen Renee Berry and Mark Lloyd Taylor. All rights reserved. Printed in the United States of America. No part of this book may be used or reproduced in any manner whatsoever without written permission except in the case of brief quotations embodied in critical articles and reviews. For information address Harper & Row, Publishers, Inc., 10 East 53rd Street, New York, NY 10022.

FIRST EDITION   TEXT DESIGN BY ADRIANE BOSWORTH

Library of Congress Cataloging in Publication Data
Berry, Carmen Renee
    Loving yourself as your neighbor : A recovery guide for Christians escaping burnout and codependency / Carmen Renee Berry & Mark Lloyd Taylor—1st ed.
        p.   cm.
    Includes bibliographical references.
    ISBN 0-06-060782-3
    1.   Burnout (Psychology)—Religious aspects—Christianity.
    2.   Helping behavior—Religious aspects—Christianity. I.   Taylor, Mark Lloyd.
    II.   Title
    BV4509.5T395   1990
    248.8′6—dc20   89-45955
                                                             CIP

90 91 92 93 94 RRD(H) 10 9 8 7 6 5 4 3 2 1

Dedicated to

Mark's grandmother, Elizabeth B. Jones,
whose faith and gifts as a writer have always served as examples,

and

in memory of Carmen's grandmother, Mary E. Hayslip,
who passed on the wisdom to live one day at a time,
the stamina to love regardless of the risk
and, when it is time, the courage to say goodbye.

Contents

Acknowledgments

We are grateful for the significant contributions many people have made to the development of this work.

We want to thank the Department of Social Work at Eastern Nazarene College in Quincy, Massachusetts, and the New England Chapter of the Association of Nazarenes in Social Work for inviting us both to speak at a conference entitled "Serving and Surviving," held in June 1988. The idea for the book was conceived at that conference.

Special appreciation is extended to Tim Lanham, A.C.S.W., and Wayne Dunlop, A.C.S.W., for their critique of the material as it was being developed, as well for their personal support and outrageous senses of humor.

Several people kindly provided Carmen with a haven in which to write: Father Edward Bernal, Deacon James Raso and Father Stuart Juleen of Saint Ann's Church in San Antonio, Texas; Michael Christensen and Rebecca Laird; and Vance Sanders, Jim Schlenker, David Clausen, Don Ensign, and Holly Kirkpatrick of His House, with special appreciation to Dr. Joel Miller.

Hugs for all the staff, members, and friends of Church of the Covenant in Boston, Massachusetts, and Trinity United Methodist Church in Poughkeepsie, New York, for being communities of love that nurtured Mark and his family in recent years. Special thanks and love to Rev. rose ann olmstead for her strong, tenacious love, her prayers, and her sermons on the sabbath principle, which helped a whole community learn to acknowledge and escape burnout; to Rev. Mick Comstock for many cups of coffee, many hours of conversation, and his sermons on the perspective of plenty; and to Rev. Toby Gould for consistent, unobtrusive caring and his gift of disclosing the spiritual riches of the communion liturgy.

For personal support throughout this process, we want to thank Patricia Luehrs, Bobette Buster, Catherine Smith, Robert Parsons, Joe Palacios, Dan Psaute, Joanne Feldmeth, Irene Flores, Michael Malloy, Tom and Marilyn Haverly, Floyd and Cindy Nease, Mick and Linda Comstock, Deborah, Rachel, and Rebekah Taylor.

We give special thanks to Roy M. Carlisle, for reading and critiquing the various versions of this manuscript.

We deeply appreciate the assistance, support, and insight we received from our editor, Jan Johnson. Her assistant, Steve Anderson, was especially helpful in pulling together the various details of the project. An additional word of thanks is due Rebecca Laird for her editorial assistance in developing the manuscript.

Loving Yourself as
Your Neighbor

Introduction

Carmen's Story

As a woman raised in an evangelical denomination, I was, from infancy, surrounded by teachings on God, love, and service. I cannot recall a time when God was not a person in my life, someone accessible and caring. Throughout my growing up years and into adulthood, serving God was a primary focus. I had committed my life to Christ and was serving God in every way I could.

In 1985, however, I suffered a serious burnout experience. I felt I was doing everything right and yet my whole life was falling apart. Depression and anxiety haunted my nights, relentless obligations and responsibilities plagued my days. I seemed unable to say no to any request for help and found myself physically ill and emotionally distraught. Eventually I could fake it no longer, and I admitted defeat. Unable to face another day giving to others when I had nothing for myself, I left my job and started therapy.

During the following year, I described my experience in the book *When Helping You Is Hurting Me: Escaping the Messiah Trap*. I had begun to understand that I was addicted to helping, what some call codependency. But there was more healing for me to experience—especially in the spiritual arena.

In the summer of 1988, I was invited to present the keynote address at a conference entitled "Serving and Surviving" sponsored by the Association of Nazarenes in Social Work, New England chapter. The conference, held at Eastern Nazarene College, had drawn a large number of professional care givers with the topic of burnout prevention. How can we serve and survive? Why were so many social workers, ministers, and lay people burning out in service to others?

After giving a presentation on my book, I settled in with the other participants at the conference to listen to a theologian named Dr. Mark Lloyd Taylor. As Mark presented on this warm June day, I was amazed by what I heard. Mark's work on the issue of love and how our distorted views of God can set us up for a helpaholic way of life struck home for me. I had struggled with my own misconceptions of God and love but had never been able to put the dilemma, or the solution, into concise words. Mark clarified what had been in the shadows for me. I could see how Mark's insights could be combined with my work regarding burnout and codependency to illuminate the trap into which so many Christians have fallen—the Messiah Trap. Many of us act as if, to be Christlike, it is our job to save the world. Mark clearly pointed out that at the heart of the Messiah Trap is spiritual distortion—of God and of love.

As we spoke after the presentation, it became clear to both of us that we shared a genuine love for our God and that our experiences and insights were compatible and potentially helpful. As a result, we combined our efforts and developed the following material.

Mark's Story

Of all things, it was an Easter egg hunt that forced me to admit that I was burned out in my volunteer activities at church. I served on one board, three committees, and an ad hoc task force. I was assistant treasurer for a year. I led worship, preached, taught child and adult Christian education classes. Somewhere along the line, I began to notice that I no longer visited with any of my friends at the coffee hour after worship. Instead, I went to meetings or chaired meetings or spent time frantically trying to get some other church business done. Eventually, I began to dread going to church—a church that had helped my wife Deborah and me turn our spiritual journeys around—because I knew some work or responsibility was there waiting for me.

But it was the Easter egg hunt that did me in. There in the splendor of neo-Gothic architecture, Tiffany stained-glass windows, awe-inspiring organ music, great preaching; there on *the* day of all days in the Christian year, the celebration of our Lord's resurrection, I found myself unable to give twenty minutes to hide Easter eggs for the children when asked by my wife. I felt physically ill when I thought of doing that one more thing. My body was saying, "No! Enough is enough," when the rest of me couldn't or wouldn't set limits. Knowing that I would hurt both Deborah's feelings and those of the children, I walked out of the sanctuary and wandered around Boston's Back Bay until the Easter egg hunt was over.

I knew that burnout was not just a problem for lay people in their church activities. Many of my friends were in human service jobs with very difficult populations. And the reason these people were working with Haitian refugees or street people or battered women was their faith in God. They considered their work a continuation of the mission of Jesus Christ in the world. And yet I heard them speak of burnout.

In the midst of my own inability to say no, to set realistic limits on my time and energy, there were always resources in my family and in my church for release and wholeness. All were embodiments of God's love for me. I love and am married to a social worker who has the incredible ability to give of herself completely to her clients and still not bring the job home with her. She has always been able to serve and survive. She gave me hope I could too.

My relationship to my wife and daughters has offered me the possibility of freedom from overcommitment. Deborah, Rachel, and Rebekah have helped me see that I am first of all Mark, a person in relationship to them. In addition, I am a teacher and a writer.

But the teaching and the writing do not make me who I am; their love for me and my love for them does.

My religious upbringing and theological education within the Wesleyan tradition also have been important resources. My parents were and are the greatest. They showed me with their lives that a relationship to God is a joyous fulfillment of our humanity, not an obligation that diminishes us as persons. John and Charles Wesley's language about the love of God has permeated my experience and my thinking. I have become convinced that the simple affirmation "God is love" really is the key to everything. If we can live this truth, and not just recite it or print it on wall hangings, we may find both the power to combat evil and a place of rest and refuge in the midst of the struggle.

When I was asked to give an address at the "Serving and Surviving" conference, I thought I would try to use the resources of God's love to address the burnout my friends and I had experienced. Listening to Carmen speak and then reading her book helped me name and tame aspects of my own burnout. Her work's practical and experiential depth seemed to complement perfectly the theological principles I was exploring. Our discovering each other at the conference impressed me as one more sign of God's love.

What Is This Book About?

The book is divided into two parts: "The Cycle of Burnout" and "The Spiral of Service." In the first part, we address factors that may set Christians up for a destructive pattern of compulsive helping or codependency. In the second part, we present a view of God's love, which can free us to care for ourselves and others in a genuinely helpful way.

Throughout the book, we follow the stories of five Christians who were caught in the Messiah Trap but escaped: Jenny, an active laywoman; Cheryl, an associate pastor; Charles, an engineering professor at a state university; Ronda, a woman whose marriage was in trouble; and Maria, a single parent.

In the first two chapters, we explain what we mean by the Messiah Trap by looking at the pain, frustration, and burnout experienced by Jenny and Cheryl. The Messiah Trap consists of two lies: (1) "If I don't do it, it won't get done"; and (2) "Everyone else's needs take priority over mine." Trapped by these two lies, Jenny tried to earn a sense of worth by acting worthy; she let others determine her actions; and she needed to overachieve. These are common characteristics of a Christian caught in the Messiah Trap. Cheryl began to exhibit other characteristics: she was attracted to helping those with pain similar to her own; she experienced difficulty in establishing peer and intimate relationships; she was caught in a cycle of isolation; she was driven to endless activity, stopping only when she dropped.

In chapter 3, we follow the stories of Charles and Maria and explore how their churches inadvertently set the Messiah Trap through the distortion of biblical teaching concerning self-denial and self-sacrifice. We also suggest that there are two perspectives from which Christians view Scripture (and life in general): the perspective of scarcity and the perspective of plenty. The perspective of scarcity says that there is not enough goodness and self-worth, especially not enough of God's love, to go around. What little there is must be carefully rationed. This perspective is typical of the Christian caught in the Messiah Trap. The challenge is to dare to believe that Jesus' perspective is not one of scarcity but that of a great banquet at which there is plenty of goodness and self-worth, especially plenty of God's love, for all.

The spiritual perspective of scarcity can be traced back to two distorted images of God, as we show in chapters 4 and 5. These images of God are created by experiences of evil and suffering in our lives. The problem lies in reconciling God's presence, activity, and goodness with the evil of this world. Cheryl faced the problem of evil when Heidi, a member of the teen group at the church Cheryl served, died of cancer. Cheryl mistakenly viewed God as an Absent Parent who did nothing about Heidi's death. Ronda encountered evil in the way she felt emotionally battered by her husband Sid and by God. Ronda experienced God as an Abusive Parent, who was always waiting to punish her for her slightest mistake.

5

These two idolatrous images of God support the two lies of the Messiah Trap. Cheryl saw God as an Absent Parent and as a result began to believe "Because God doesn't seem to be doing anything about evil, I must." This is the first lie: "If I don't do it, it won't get done." Experiencing God as an Abusive Parent, Ronda acted as if she believed, "Because God doesn't respect my value as a person, it doesn't matter if other people mistreat me too." This is the second lie of the Messiah Trap: "Everyone else's needs take priority over mine."

A solution to the problem of evil and an escape from the Messiah Trap are found in God's love. In chapter 6, we see how Charles began to make real progress when he discovered what love is. He learned to allow others to make a difference in his life and to give of himself to those others. In Charles's transformation, we discover a new image of love, one in which love has two sides: receptivity and activity.

In chapters 7 and 8, we describe how Cheryl and Ronda escaped the Messiah Trap when they discovered a new image of God as pure, unbounded love. This image of God is the biblical one, portrayed in Psalm 103; the parable of the "prodigal father" in Luke 15; and, above all, the life, death, and resurrection of Jesus of Nazareth. God's love is both receptive and active. The receptive aspect of God's pure, unbounded love proves that God is not an Absent Parent. Cheryl found that the evil of the world is not something to which God is indifferent. God suffered the evil of Heidi's death along with her. Her pain was God's pain. She began to see God as her Attentive Parent. The active side of God's pure, unbounded love reveals that God is not an Abusive Parent. Ronda discovered that God did not coerce her, control her, or treat her like a thing. Instead, God acts in love by giving her the space and support to create herself freely. God, Ronda saw, is her Nurturing Parent.

Because God really does love us, we can love ourselves appropriately. In chapter 9, we look at the story of the breakthrough in Jenny's life, which came when she believed that God was calling her to love herself as her own closest neighbor. This offered Jenny a new image of self. As she began to love herself, Jenny exhibited the characteristics of the Spiral of Service rather than those of the Messiah Trap. She began to accept the fact that God loves her just as she is; she took the time and effort to care for herself; and she was able to set realistic goals and limits.

God's love also makes possible a new image of the church, as we see in chapter 10. When we experience God as our Attentive and Nurturing Parent, our churches can become what they ought to be, communities of love. All relationships in the church are to be seen as the relationships between beloved ones. Maria's life was transformed when she became a part of such a community of beloved ones. She found herself unconditionally accepted and gently supported.

Finally, in chapter 11, we see how Charles was able to live on the Spiral of Service. He was able to give in love to others without burning himself out. Charles reversed the characteristics of the Christian caught in the Messiah Trap. He was able to: relate to others with the receptivity and activity of love; establish, protect, and nurture peer and intimate relationships; belong to the group and retain a sense of self; take satisfaction in a job well done; and problem-solve effectively.

PART One

The Cycle of Burnout

CHAPTER 1

Have You Fallen into the Messiah Trap?

There is no fear in love, but perfect love casts out fear. For fear has to do with punishment, and whoever fears is not perfected in love.
—1 John 4:18

Jenny closed the door after the last person in the Bible study left. No longer able to hold back the tears, she leaned against the door and wept. "What is wrong with me, anyway?" she scolded herself, but the tears flowed undaunted. "Why am I so miserable when I am trying to do everything right?"

Jenny, like so many Christians, was trying her best to live out her love for God. As a committed Christian, she attended church regularly with her husband and two teenage daughters. Vivacious and outgoing, Jenny served on several committees, taught a weekly Bible study, and volunteered for a variety of tasks. Each week it seemed like someone else asked for her help and each week Jenny always said yes.

Lately, it was getting harder and harder to keep up with the demands of her busy schedule. Her vitality was being depleted. Out of desperation, she had tried to resign from one of her committees. Ed, the committee chairperson, had responded, "But Jenny, we need you on that committee. We have no one to replace you. Can't you serve just one more term?" Jenny had buckled under the pressure and the guilt, but she was starting to pay the price. Recently, she had developed terrible headaches, so painful at times that she had to cancel all her appointments and stay in bed.

Jenny walked slowly into the living room to straighten up after the group. "I'm so afraid, sometimes," Jenny thought to herself, "that I am failing God. I so much want to please God and do the right thing. But no matter what I do for other people, it never seems to be enough. My daughters tell me that I don't have enough time for them. People at the church are complaining and I don't blame them. I just can't seem to keep up with all I've promised to do!"

Jenny stacked the dirty dishes in dismay. "But I don't have anything left to give. What's wrong with me? It seems to me that I should be enjoying the blessings of the Lord on my life, my work, and my spiritual growth." Jenny's shoulders slumped in defeat as she felt another headache coming on. "Well, I can't pretend any more. I am miserable. In fact, I'm so exhausted and frustrated that I don't think I can take much more of this." A flash of anger crossed her weary face. "What does God want from me, anyway?"

Falling into the Messiah Trap

Have you fallen into the Messiah Trap? Are you giving but never receiving, obeying but never questioning, listening but never being heard? The Messiah Trap allows no time for personal pursuits, solitude, or fun. People who fall into the Messiah Trap no longer have the word *no* in their vocabularies. They feel compelled to answer every call for help.

Our use of the term *Messiah Trap* needs explanation. As Christians, we believe that Jesus of Nazareth is the true Messiah, the one chosen and anointed by God to save people from their brokenness and sin. Through his teaching, healing, death, and resurrection, Jesus the Messiah brings to us the powerful presence of God. Only Jesus, we believe, is worthy of being called "Messiah" in the true sense.

The Christian faith asserts that Jesus was both fully human and fully divine. Jesus, the Messiah, had both the capacity and the right to die for the forgiveness and healing of a sinful world. Because of Jesus' death and resurrection, we are able to come into relationship with a loving God.

We, on the other hand, are not divine. We are not God's Messiah, God's anointed one. While we are called to follow Jesus' example of love in all we do, we are not called to pretend to be divine. Unfortunately, we sometimes confuse being Christlike with playing the role of God in other people's lives. This is the Messiah Trap.

The Messiah Trap is comprised of two lies: (1) *If I don't do it, it won't get done;* and (2) *Everyone else's needs take priority over mine.* The first lie is based on an unrealistic sense of our responsibility. When we fall into the Messiah Trap, we act *as if* we were the true Messiah. Mistakenly, we act as if we were individually responsible for and had to sacrifice ourselves for the sake of the entire world. Jenny fell into the Messiah Trap when she began to believe that she was indispensable, the only one who could lead the Bible study, the only one who could help those who claimed to need her. Jenny felt trapped because she did not yet understand that God was calling her to love, not to codependency and burnout.

The second lie of the Messiah Trap is "Everyone else's needs take priority over mine." Once Jenny took on the Messiah Trap way of life, she sacrificed her own peace of mind, her relationship with her daughters, and even her health. Why? Because she saw her own legitimate needs as secondary. Many Christians demand this level of sacrifice as evidence of their spiritual commitment. As a result, these dedicated people never take time for themselves. Once in the Messiah Trap, burnout is sure to follow.

For human beings like ourselves to play the role of God is masochistic, even blasphemous. The result is always the same: self-destruction. A Christian caught in the Messiah Trap pretends to be God and, in the process, is crushed as a human being. Trapped by the lies, we fail to open ourselves to the abundant life Jesus, the true Messiah, offers.

How Do We Fall into the Messiah Trap?

As Christians, we believe that God longs to be in relationship with us and sent Jesus, the true Messiah, to make this relationship possible. When we see God clearly, we can experience God loving us, attending to us, and nurturing our growth. As a result, we are moved naturally to a place of intimacy with God, with ourselves, and with others. When we hold a distorted view of God, however, we can be set up to fall into the Messiah Trap. Two distorted views of God, which will be explored in depth later, are *God is absent* and *God is abusive.*

When we view God as absent, we become snared by the first lie of the Messiah Trap: "If I don't do it, it won't get done." While we might give lip service to a God who is an active participant in our lives, we actually live as if God were absent. As a consequence, we find ourselves on a treadmill of activity, desperately trying to fill God's shoes. Of course, we will fail.

On the other hand, those of us who believe God is abusive fall prey to the second lie of the Messiah Trap: "Everyone else's needs take priority over mine." While we may say God loves us, we secretly fear that God is watching our every move, ready to pounce on us if we make a mistake. We live as if God were fickle, rigid, and demanding, a judge to be feared, not an advocate to be trusted. As a result, we feel obligated to go, not just the extra mile, but far beyond what is humanly possible. Our sacrifice is often great, but the result is always disappointing.

When, in spite of our best efforts, things go wrong, we Messiahs rarely question our assumptions about God. Rather, we falsely believe that peace of mind has evaded us because we haven't done enough, aren't good enough, aren't committed enough, aren't "mature in our faith." The Messiah Trap takes everything we have and leaves us confused, alienated, enraged, and burned out. Falling into the Messiah Trap can cost us everything we have and everyone we love.

If we do not know who God really is, we cannot know who we really are. How can we embrace our genuine worth when we feel God is inaccessible to us? How can we trust that we are lovable when we feel battered by an abusive God? Our distorted views of God send us on a fruitless search for who we really are.

Those caught in the Messiah Trap often struggle with three major problem areas in their lives. A Christian caught in the Messiah Trap is someone who

1. tries to earn a sense of worth by "acting" worthy;
2. lets others determine his or her actions; and
3. needs to overachieve.

1. Tries to Earn a Sense of Worth by "Acting" Worthy

One Monday night, as usual, Jenny was preparing for her Bible study, which would meet the next evening. This particular lesson, on salvation by grace through faith in Christ alone, troubled her. She secretly feared that she didn't have enough faith and didn't deserve God's grace and forgiveness. When Jenny was actively involved in helping others, this fear would subside. But when she found herself unable to keep up the pace, she would become quite fearful again.

Most of us who have fallen into the Messiah Trap are keenly aware of our failings. In fact, we not only feel guilty about what we have done or left undone, we feel ashamed of who we are. When we first turned to God, we found love, acceptance, and forgiveness through Jesus Christ.

"When I first accepted Christ," Jenny thought to herself with eyes aglow, "I was elated and filled with an enthusiasm for life. The change in me was so marvelous! Instead of feeling resentful, there was gratitude for God's love. I, of all people, didn't deserve that love. All I wanted to do was please God."

Jenny had plunged head first into her new life, excitedly meeting new people at church, volunteering for anything anyone would let her do. It was not long before her congregation recognized her many talents and included her in more and more activities. With her husband and daughters beside her on the pew, Jenny could not imagine how anything could spoil her happiness.

But somewhere along the way, Jenny had lost this sense of gratitude. Staring down at her Bible, she tried to recall, "When did it happen? Where did the joy go?" The Scriptures that once comforted her now filled her with fear. Her enthusiasm was replaced by a dreaded sense of obligation. Unable to keep up the pace, Jenny now doubted that God loved her, and, perhaps most damaging of all, she began to believe she needed to earn God's love. She fell into the Messiah Trap when she stopped relying on God's love as an undeserved gift and tried to earn her worth by an addictive codependent lifestyle filled with "helpful" activities.

2. Lets Others Determine His or Her Actions

At the store one day, Jenny ran into Kit, one of her friends from back in school. Kit asked if they could get together for dinner sometime to go over the good old days. Jenny looked at her calendar and, because of commitments at church, she didn't have a free evening for several weeks. Jenny saw the flash of disappointment in her friend's eyes as Kit made a joke and walked away.

The Messiah Trap tells us that although we are unworthy sinners, we can earn God's love and approval by living a "Christian" life (the first lie) and that we must do so by helping others in a way that puts our needs last (the second lie). Jenny wanted desperately to feel secure in God's love and would have done just about anything for that security. And that's exactly what she did; she did whatever anyone else wanted her to do. Her time and energy were no longer her own.

Once we fall into the Messiah Trap, we lose control over our lives. We no longer decide how and with whom we spend our time. Instead, we find ourselves frantically trying to fulfill the expectations of others. We spend our time with whomever claims to need us the most. This may sound like an exaggeration, but, be assured, it is not. When caught in the Messiah Trap, we become consumed with an addiction to helping. Like Jenny, we soon have no life beyond our helping, codependent activities.

Jenny prided herself on the fact that whenever the doors of the church were open, she was always there. Rarely a day or evening went by that she wasn't involved in some activity, whether it was attending services, leading weekly study groups, or providing transportation for the teen program. Even on Saturdays, she visited the elderly. Jenny was a woman who never said no.

"I feel pulled in so many directions!" Jenny complained to herself, unwilling to tell anyone else about her struggle. "Everyone wants a piece of me and I have tried. I really have tried. It's strange that the more I try, the less I seem to please other people. I feel out of control, like a roller coaster about to jump track."

3. Needs to Overachieve

Jenny had worked for weeks designing the brochure for the Easter pageant. She wanted everything to be just right. After several thousand copies of the brochure had been printed and mailed, one of the deacons complained that his name was misspelled. For the next several weeks Jenny felt humiliated, resentful, and angry at herself.

Trying to earn salvation, self-worth, and God's love is no easy task. To accomplish this, one would have to be flawless, sinless, and perfect. One would have to be God. Only Jesus, the true Messiah, has been able to claim those characteristics. And yet the Messiah Trap fools us into thinking that we too can achieve perfection on our own merit.

Jenny, like so many caught up in the Messiah Trap, did not recognize the impossibility of the task. She was aware, however, of how fearful she felt of making a mistake and how deeply wounded she felt when criticized. Jenny mused, "I tried so hard on those brochures. It was the first time I had tried my hand at artwork and design. But the most important thing to me was that everyone who had contributed to the Easter pageant was included in the brochure. I checked the spelling of those names over and over again. But one got past me." As she slumped further into the chair, Jenny sighed. "It was a failure. I never should have tried."

Those of us caught in the Messiah Trap have no middle ground. Doing "enough" is never enough. We are either perfect (and therefore secure in God's love) or failures (and in danger of losing our souls). Failure or success. Sin or righteousness. Hell or heaven. With each task we perform, we put our very souls on the line.

Sometimes Messiahs focus on the *quality* of their accomplishments, and at other times they may emphasize the *quantity* of the tasks they take on. Jenny was the kind of person who could never say no and prided herself on the large number of helping activities in which she participated. In addition to this heavy load, Jenny wanted everything she did to be perfect.

Trying to cheer herself up, Jenny thought, "Why am I getting so upset about one typo? I didn't mean to slight that guy. Certainly there's room for a little human error, isn't there?" Jenny quietly pondered her statement. "It's no use, I can't talk myself out of it. I messed up and I really feel awful."

The Impossible Task

The bad news is that trying to earn our worth is impossible. The good news is that it is also unnecessary. God loves us as we are. All we need to do is accept that fact. When our understanding of God becomes distorted, however, we inevitably come to doubt both God's love for us and our own intrinsic worth as persons. We become sidetracked into a way of life that, on the surface, may seem godly, but is actually a distortion of love.

CHAPTER 2

Are You on Fire or Burning Out?

If I speak in the tongues of human beings and of angels, but have not love, I am a noisy gong or a clanging cymbal. And if I have prophetic powers, and understand all mysteries and all knowledge, and if I have all faith, so as to remove mountains, but have not love, I am nothing. If I give away all I have, and if I deliver my body to be burned, but have not love, I gain nothing."
—1 Corinthians 13:1–3

Sitting in her counselor's office, Cheryl clung to her appointment book as if it were a life preserver and she were lost at sea. An associate pastor at a large church, she tackled the daily demands with the conviction that hers was more than "just a job."

"For me," she explained, "my work is a calling from God. I know this is what God wants me to do with my life, but," her voice broke momentarily, "there are times I feel so, so alone. I try to pray but it feels like no one is listening. Everyone relies on me at church, so I haven't known who to turn to with my own problems.

"Several months back," Cheryl continued, "Katie, one of our youth workers, noticed I was down and asked what was troubling me. I was so relieved that I started telling her about my frustration and doubts. And you know what she said?" Cheryl asked, not expecting an answer. "She patted me on the arm and told me the best way to feel better about my own problems is to help someone else. Then she said that I'd feel better if I were around young people. So, in addition to my other duties, I also volunteered to work with the youth."

"Did that make you feel better?" the counselor asked.

"It did at first. These kids are so full of life and enthusiasm! But soon the additional work load began to wear me out even further. And being a teenager these days is not easy. I didn't have many answers for these young people."

Cheryl struggled as if there were more to tell, but she was having trouble finding the words. "There's just so much pain. Heidi, one of the honor teenagers, a young, beautiful girl with such potential, was recently diagnosed with terminal cancer. We were all devastated." Cheryl shook her head slowly. "So instead of feeling better, I just feel bad for Heidi and guilty for my own feelings of despair."

While the idea of helping others is one that all Christians should value, it is critical to see that Katie actually encouraged Cheryl to use helping as a *narcotic,* as a means to numb herself to her own pain. Rather than go before God to understand her feelings better, Cheryl was encouraged to close her ears to what God may have been telling her and to repress legitimate feelings. Such advice would have seemed obviously harmful if Cheryl had been told that she would feel better if she drank a shot of whiskey or snorted a line of cocaine. But whether the addictive substance is alcohol or the addictive process is helping, the effect is the same. We become cut off from our true feelings while our mood and perceptions are altered by drinking, snorting, ingesting—or helping—in an addictive, codependent fashion. And, as in all addictions, the high never lasts.

Unknowingly, Katie was setting up her friend Cheryl for the Messiah Trap. Rather than spend time listening to Cheryl and supporting her in her feelings, Katie was encouraging Cheryl to "do" instead of to "be." Because Cheryl fell into this trap, she began to exhibit several of the Messiah characteristics.

A Christian caught in the Messiah Trap is someone who

1. is attracted to helping those with similar pain;
2. experiences difficulty in establishing peer and intimate relationships;
3. is caught in a cycle of isolation;
4. is driven to endless activity; and
5. stops when he or she drops.

1. Is Attracted to Helping Those with Similar Pain

Although Cheryl was warm with all of the teens in the youth group, Heidi had won Cheryl's heart. From the first day they had met, Cheryl felt a special love for this young, vivacious girl. Now, at the sound of Cheryl's hello, Heidi would raise herself from the hospital bed and her drawn face would pull into a grin. Heidi seemed so alone and fragile that it was hard for Cheryl to leave after each visit. She had the impulse to sweep Heidi up in her arms and take her home.

As we have listened to many people who have fallen into the Messiah Trap, one factor seems common to all. Each person carries deep within a hurt, often acquired in childhood, that is unresolved and unattended. Part of the lie of the Messiah Trap is that there is no time for addressing our own needs and hurts. Dealing with our own pain, we are led to believe, would be selfish. To be selfish, so the lie goes, is to be imperfect, and to be imperfect is to be unworthy of God's love.

Tears welled up in Cheryl's eyes as she confessed to her counselor, "I have never felt loved. Even though I try to act confident and competent, underneath I feel like a frightened little girl."

Cheryl's father had left her and her mother when Cheryl was a child. Her mother always seemed to be either working or sleeping.

"I only remember her being cranky with me. I never could please her."

Wiping her eyes, Cheryl recalled, "One day when I was in the fourth grade, I had written a story about our cat Fluffy. My teacher had it printed in the school newspaper. Was I ever proud! I was so excited, I fairly flew the two blocks home from school, bounded up to the top floor of our triple decker, and burst through the door of the apartment. Mom was lying on the couch.

"She snarled at me, 'Can't you be quiet! You sounded like a herd of elephants coming up those stairs!' I told her I was sorry, then asked her if I could read my story. She said 'You know Mr. Sullivan sleeps during the day. You'll wake him up and he'll have the landlord over in a jiffy to throw you out in the street.'

"I thought she hadn't heard me, so I took out the school newspaper and showed her the story with my name above it. She looked shocked. 'You? You wrote a story? You know you can't spell, never could. I hope they checked the spelling before they printed it.' I was heartbroken. She slowly dragged herself off the couch and slumped toward the stove. 'Go ahead,' she said impatiently, 'read me the story while I make some coffee. I've gotta wake up and get to the Lowell Building to do those floors. All of them need waxing.'

"So I started reading about Fluffy—how she looked out the window, twitching all over, watching the squirrels on the fire escape. As I read, my mother banged the tea kettle under the faucet, ran the water, filling up the kettle. With a splash, the kettle plopped down on the stove. A match snarled, the gas puffed and ignited. Then my mother walked to the pantry, out of earshot, and began rummaging for the instant coffee and a cup and a spoon and the sugar and a new can of evaporated milk and a can opener.

"Right in the middle of the sentence about Fluffy's weekly game of hide and seek in the empty shopping bags, the best sentence in the story, I could stand it no longer. Quietly, with hot tears on my face, I retreated to my room. And you know, my mother never asked me how the story about Fluffy ended."

"Has anyone else ever asked you about yourself, about your problems?" the counselor inquired.

Cheryl sat in stunned silence. "Now that you ask, I can't think of anyone who encouraged me to talk about my own feelings. The people at the church were caring and supportive of me, unlike my mother. But the emphasis there was on helping others, not helping myself. I guess I just tried to go on as if nothing had ever hurt me. It was easier to pretend to be strong."

As Cheryl was discovering, the hurts we have hidden deep within us do not go away because we ignore them. Instead, they will fester, plaguing us with feelings we don't understand. Often we will find ourselves unconsciously attracted to other people who share our pain. Cheryl was drawn to Heidi because this young woman reflected her own feelings of loneliness, uselessness, and vulnerability. Often those caught in the Messiah Trap mistake such feelings for love. But do not be fooled, the attraction is based on our own neediness, not the strength of love.

Cheryl's experience is common for those caught in the Messiah Trap. Unused to feeling her own pain, Cheryl learned to feel Heidi's. Unable to care for her own needs, Cheryl nurtured her young friend. Unwilling to make time to care for herself directly, Cheryl always made time for Heidi. In fact, Cheryl had begun to visit the hospital daily, saying that Heidi could pass away at any time. Although the motivation was unconscious, when Cheryl cared for Heidi, it was in response to the reflection Cheryl saw of herself in Heidi's eyes. Heidi became Cheryl's primary access to herself. Caring for Heidi became an obsession.

2. Experiences Difficulty in Establishing Peer and Intimate Relationships

Cheryl stared down at the letter in her hand, a letter from John, the man she had been dating. "I would have told you in person that I was seeing someone else, but you've been so busy that you never seemed to have the time to talk. I'm sorry, but I need someone who has time for me."

"That letter made no sense to me at the time," Cheryl confessed. "How could John be jealous of a teenage girl in a hospital? Sure, the hours I put into my ministry were long. But I just couldn't understand how he could have felt neglected. After all, when he first met me he told me he was attracted by my commitment to the ministry. Then he leaves me because of my devotion to Heidi. Well, I certainly didn't feel like I had anything more to give!"

There is no place for genuine intimacy in the Messiah Trap; no place, no time, no energy. Cheryl was so driven by her unidentified needs that she never allowed time to have those needs met. She tried so hard to *earn* God's love that she had no time to *experience* God's love. In the same way, she was so busy trying to earn John's love that she could not accept the relationship John freely offered. Life was squeezed out and love was squelched.

Cheryl mistook addictive, codependent helping for genuine loving. Many Christians caught in the Messiah Trap have this problem. We do not have to look far to see those who are busy with everyone else's needs but their own and their loved ones. Many people, sometimes ministers or missionaries, lead such busy lives that their spouses are starved for affection and their children are aching for attention. These people are devout in their faith and committed to their spouses, yet their marriages often wither and die from neglect. When their children need attention, these parents are attending to the needs of those to whom they minister. Often the children in these families grow up to be angry, resentful, and rejecting of God. It should come as no surprise since these children were neglected in the name of God.

The people Cheryl claimed to love the most were usually the ones who got the least attention. It is ironic but a common experience for those of us caught in the Messiah Trap. We do not take time for ourselves, and, in a similar fashion, we neglect those closest to us. Some stay and suffer from neglect. Others, like John, turn away to find love elsewhere, leaving the Messiah alone and confused.

3. Is Caught in a Cycle of Isolation

Leaning back in her chair, Cheryl let the debate of the church board meeting drone on without her. As she looked around the table, she saw a room full of faces, many of which she had known for years. And yet there was no one she could talk to, not really, at least not about the fears she'd been having lately. Worrying about Heidi's impending death, Cheryl had been having nightmares about dying and not being ready to meet God. Where could she turn? Who would understand?

Cheryl knew that Heidi was very weak and frail. Each afternoon, Cheryl was anxious to return and see her friend, quietly dreading the day she would come and find Heidi gone. Late one night, Cheryl received a phone call. She jumped out of bed and was able to make it to the hospital in time to hold the girl's hand one more time. Still able to recognize Cheryl's voice, Heidi smiled tenderly and then slipped into the next world.

Even though Cheryl had tried to prepare herself for Heidi's death, she still felt as if her world had broken in two. Tears filled Cheryl's eyes as she recalled, "I was in shock after Heidi died. There was something about her, like we shared a secret or something. When she died, it felt like a part of me had died." When Heidi passed away, Cheryl lost more than a close friend. She also lost access to herself.

Like Cheryl, we Christians often begin our spiritual journeys by experiencing the loving forgiveness of God. How is it that we may now feel so alone and in such danger? Like Cheryl, all of us caught in the Messiah Trap end up feeling isolated and fearful of letting anyone know who we really are.

"You know," Cheryl confided, "I actually tried to talk about my problems one more time. After a meeting, out in the parking lot, I commented to Katie that I didn't feel like I was a very good Christian. 'You?' she looked surprised, 'Why, Cheryl, you're the most faithful Christian we have in the congregation! If you're not right with God, then no one is.' And with that Katie drove off." Shaking her head sadly, Cheryl concluded, "It was no use. I felt that no one at the church or in my family understood what I was going through."

4. Is Driven to Endless Activity

Realizing that Cheryl was taking Heidi's death so hard, Katie decided to help by encouraging Cheryl to get her mind off her troubles. Katie nominated Cheryl for chairperson of the district youth committee, hoping that her involvement with others less fortunate would bring Cheryl out of her depression.

Wait a minute. This sounds familiar. When Cheryl was depressed before, wasn't it Katie who encouraged her to get more involved with helping the youth? Didn't she promise Cheryl she would feel better, not worse, if she helped someone else who was less fortunate? If it didn't work then, why would anyone think it would work now?

This is the cycle of burnout caused by the Messiah Trap. We are given promises that never come true. Then the failures are blamed on us. We are told that we didn't try hard enough or long enough, but, if we try again, *this* time we'll achieve all that we desire.

"I tried to tell Katie that I had no more energy left," Cheryl anxiously wrung her hands. "She just wouldn't listen and said that getting out with other people is what I needed and I was being selfish hoarding all this organizational talent. The next thing I knew, I was in charge of all the youth activities for the entire district!" Cheryl sighed deeply, fingering the flier highlighting the plight of the neglected youth. "There really are so many teenagers on the streets these days and I do feel that we Christians should be on the front lines helping these kids. I guess Katie is right. I'll feel better about Heidi's death and even my own spiritual doubts if I'm doing my best for the Kingdom."

5. Stops When He or She Drops

One morning Cheryl awoke and knew she couldn't face the day. It didn't matter how many appointments or responsibilities she had at the church, she knew she couldn't live this way any longer. Not knowing what else to do, she rolled over, buried her face in the pillow, and cried.

If you are caught in the Messiah Trap way, you will inevitably burn out. All addictions are built on lies and all lead to death.

We believe that 1 Corinthians 13 addresses this issue clearly and squarely. Paul writes that a person can speak in unknown tongues, prophesy, have great knowledge, possess a faith that moves mountains, give all their possessions to the poor, even offer their bodies in a martyr's death, and still gain nothing, accomplish nothing. Why? Because that person lacks love.

Ensnared in the Messiah Trap, we might try to live out our faith, attend church each week, pay our tithe, memorize Scripture, follow the church's guidelines, teach Sunday school, support relief efforts to the poor, advocate for social justice, share the gospel, all in an attempt to earn God's love. If so, all this activity is worthless. Love has nothing to do with the Messiah Trap. If caught in the Messiah Trap, we are not loving other people, we are *using* them to get at our own pain. *Messiah-style helping, even in the name of Christ, is still an addiction.* Do not be fooled. Without love, all that we do and all that we are adds up to nothing and results in death.

Staring at her Bible, Cheryl's eyes filled with sad tears. "As I read over this passage in First Corinthians, it hurts to admit it, but I don't really know how to love anyone. I want to please God, but it's more like performing for a demanding taskmaster than responding in gratitude and love." She sighed, "And then to realize that all my effort has been for nothing. Nothing at all!"

A sad smile crept across her tired face. "You know, it's beginning to make sense to me now, why all the trying never got me anywhere. I'm actually relieved to find out it isn't because I'm a failure or because God is punishing me somehow. I've been caught up in a powerful addiction. It's time to admit that I have fallen into the Messiah Trap."

CHAPTER 3

How Does the Church Set the Messiah Trap?

For I desire steadfast love and not sacrifice, the knowledge of God, rather than burnt offerings.
—Hosea 6:6

The church is meant to be a place where people can find freedom from all types of addictive and destructive ways of living, including addictions to helping and codependency. The preaching, liturgy, education programs, pastoral care and counseling, and fellowship of the church ought to embody God's love to heal and bring release from the Messiah Trap. Sometimes, however, the church is part of the problem rather than part of the solution. Sometimes sermons, worship, Christian education lessons, counseling, and relationships among church members help to set the Messiah Trap. The result is pain, frustration, anger, and guilt.

One way the church sets the Messiah Trap, we believe, is by misinterpreting biblical teaching about self-sacrifice and self-denial. Biblical passages on sacrifice have an important message for all of us. The Christian life is indeed one of service, as we will see later in this book. But there is a difference between the Spiral of Service based on love and the Cycle of Burnout experienced by the Christian caught in the Messiah Trap. When Christians misinterpret the self-sacrifice and self-denial passages, we no longer serve as Jesus Christ served. Instead, we act addictively and codependently, from which Jesus came to free us. Jesus offers freedom from the bondage of addictive helping. But before we can appreciate the freedom Jesus offers, we need to examine more closely the way his teaching has been distorted.

Love, Not Sacrifice

Charles taught engineering at a large state university. A well-liked teacher and an active member in his professional society, Charles was conscientious in his work. He said yes to everything he was asked to do, fulfilling more obligations than most of his colleagues. But even though Charles accepted these many assignments, he found little joy in his involvement. He felt frustrated that he never had time to complete each task the way he would have liked.

Remembering those days, Charles said, "I was always rushing ten minutes before a committee meeting to finish my report and to get it photocopied." He grinned, "I cannot recall a morning I didn't wake up feeling the pressure of all the work that the day would bring me. It was always hanging over my head—the tests to grade, the laboratory exercises to write, the committee work to finish, the grant proposals to draft. Oh, it was a terrible burden!"

Not only was Charles overextended at work, he also took on a variety of responsibilities at church. "I served on the parish council and the stewardship committee. I also taught an occasional adult Christian education class. My wife, Sara, and I had been attracted to our church because of its active outreach program to its inner city neighborhood. Our faith was centered around Jesus' teaching in Matthew 25:31–40." Turning in his Bible to a well-worn page, Charles read,

> When the Son of Man comes as King, and all the angels
> with him, then he will sit on his royal throne, and all the
> earth's people will be gathered before him. Then he will

divide them into two groups, just as a shepherd sepa-
rates the sheep from the goats: he will put the sheep at
his right and the goats on his left. Then the King will say
to the people on his right: "You who are blessed by God:
come! Come and receive the kingdom which has been
prepared for you ever since the creation of the world. I
was hungry and you fed me, thirsty and you gave me
drink; I was a stranger and you received me in your
homes, naked and you clothed me; I was sick and you
took care of me, in prison and you visited me." The righ-
teous will then answer him: "When, Lord, did we ever
see you hungry and feed you, or thirsty and give you
drink? When did we ever see you a stranger and welcome you into our homes, or naked and clothe you?
When did we ever see you sick or in prison, and visit
you?" Then the King will answer back, "I tell you, indeed, whenever you did this for one of these poorest
brothers and sisters of mine, you did it for me!" (TEV)

With a serious commitment to illustrating his love for God
through caring for others, Charles unintentionally fell into the
Messiah Trap. By mistaking codependency for the genuine expression of love, Charles became ensnared in the first lie of the Messiah
Trap, "If I don't do it, it won't get done."

"To say no to a request for assistance," Charles explained, "felt
like saying no to God. I became obsessed with proving my love for
God by helping every person I met." Charles felt that God demanded that he prove his love by saying yes to everyone who
wanted something from him. "As a result, I was exhausted."

Charles continued, "I remember one Sunday when I was feeling especially low and overwhelmed. I had been thinking about
resigning some of my duties to make more time for myself. We
were at the end of a special series of adult Christian education lessons on the church's mission to the world. The speaker that final
Sunday had been a successful physician in private practice in the
United States. She told the story of a dramatic turnaround in her
life, which led her to leave her practice, sell her home and cars, and

31

go to East Africa to work in a refugee clinic sponsored by the United Nations.

"I can see now that what the doctor did was right for her. I believe God calls people to go out on a limb, make a break with their comfortable lifestyles, and help others. Her mission to East Africa was courageous and faithful. There are times that we need to be challenged to stretch ourselves." Charles sighed deeply. "But her message, however sincere, had a negative impact on me at that point in my life. I wasn't complacent. To the contrary, I was already doing too much. My work and my volunteer activities had become obsessions. I did not need to *do* more. I needed to learn how to love."

Charles shook his head. "The doctor closed her presentation by saying, 'We must follow Jesus' call to deny ourselves. We Americans have so much and the rest of the world has so little. What gives me the right to be rich and the rest of the world be poor?' She quoted Mark 8:34–35 where Jesus says, 'If anyone would come after me, let them deny themselves and take up their cross and follow me. For whoever would save their life will lose it; and whoever loses their life for my sake and the gospel's will save it.' "

The doctor's presentation made Charles feel extremely guilty. He felt guilty about his prosperity in a world of poor people. "After the lesson," Charles continued, "I was just sitting in the corner of the room, feeling ashamed of being alive, when the director of our ministry to the homeless came up and asked me to participate in the program. Of course, I said yes."

"It is hard for me to admit, even now," confessed Charles, "that I helped, not out of love but because I felt it was my duty. How would God know of my love if I didn't help these people? It was more like an act of atonement for my privileged place in the world. I was trying to apologize for who I was. I believed that Jesus was ashamed of me, too, and that was why I was to 'lose' myself in the lives of others. I actually began to despise myself and see myself as evil."

Motivated by guilt, shame, and a sense of duty, Charles volunteered to work one lunch hour a week in the church's meals program for the homeless. He believed that this self-sacrifice would please God and provide him with the peace of mind he so desperately needed. But rather than experiencing a sense of belonging, Charles felt alone and disconnected. "It never occurred to me to question my motivation," he said. "I figured that I was miserable because I wasn't doing enough. So I volunteered for two lunch hours a week. When that wasn't satisfying, I added Saturdays. Before I knew it, I was there nearly every day. I became consumed with this ministry."

An addiction promises satisfaction but never delivers it. The more Charles gave, the emptier he felt. The more Charles sacrificed, the more guilt he suffered. He seemed to be losing his life but not regaining it. He was denying himself but never being replenished. Charles's pattern of burnout was a major signal that he had fallen into the Messiah Trap. Christ's death was followed by the resurrection. When our sacrifices are followed by rebirth and renewal, we can be confident that we are following in Christ's footsteps. But when we offer ourselves in sacrifice and are left battered, confused, and depleted, we are not loving as Christ loved. We are caught in the Messiah Trap.

"My misguided motivation became painfully apparent to me one Saturday afternoon," Charles remembered. "It was my job to oversee the whole operation and, with another volunteer, cook and clean up. It was a particularly miserable afternoon, with a cold, hard rain driving everyone into the fellowship hall of the church. It was more crowded that usual. The street people were wet and irritable, ready for a hot meal.

"As I walked in, I found a note on the kitchen door saying that my co-worker had been called out of town on a family emergency. To make matters worse, I looked over the food supply and realized we were going to be at least twenty meals short." Charles hurriedly made a half dozen phone calls trying to round up some more food. The best he could do was several buckets of fried chicken donated by a local fast food place. "And did I get any thanks? No way. Just complaints that everyone didn't get the same meal."

Charles's job was not finished once the crowd was fed. Cleaning up was especially difficult because of the muddy floors and wet hallways. "I was exhausted." Charles shoulders slumped. "After cleaning up all by myself, I pushed through the rain toward my car. And when I got there I found Sam, one of our regulars at the meals program, drenched to the bone, using the hood of my car to sort his collection of cans and bottles!" All of Charles's frustration about the day, all of the resentment and guilt, all of his burnout, became crystallized in Sam's bottles and cans.

"I screamed at him, 'You stupid moron!'" Charles recalled with sadness in his eyes. "And with a sweep of my arm, I sent the bottles and cans crashing to the pavement. I leaped into my car, started it, and sped out of the alley trailing rubber behind me. My heart was still pounding, twenty minutes later, when I got to my home in the suburbs."

When his rage finally dissipated, Charles felt foolish and ashamed. He knew that when the bottles shattered on the pavement, he had also shattered Sam's trust. What was junk to Charles seemed like prized possessions to Sam, the promise of a few dollars at the recycler that could literally mean life or death to this struggling man. Not only had he violated Sam's dignity, Charles had also damaged the church's credibility with all the street people.

But something else was shattered that afternoon: Charles's fantasy that his sacrifice had been useful and faithful. "I realized that I had been trying to salve my own guilt. I pretended that I was some noble messenger from God, reaching down to these poor, disadvantaged street people. It was sheer arrogance the way I looked down on those people and the way I tried to play god in their lives." Charles had been haunted by the first lie of the Messiah Trap: "If I don't do it, it won't get done." He had lost sight of genuine service to others and thought only of himself, the server.

The next Sunday, Charles sat in the church pew confused and humiliated by his own limitations. The pastor stood and read God's word given through the prophet Hosea, "I desire steadfast love and not sacrifice." A light began to dawn for Charles as he thought about his endless activity. "I wasn't quite sure what love was, but I knew it was not what I had been doing. I hadn't been loving Sam and the others. I had been obsessed with appearances, acting as if I were loving, as a way to earn God's approval. I was offering God plenty of sacrifice but precious little love."

No More Burnt Offerings

Maria was a single parent trying to raise three children on her meager salary as a typist in a big insurance company. She had been divorced for several years from an alcoholic husband who had drifted in and out of the home. Things had been worse while he was at home, for when he drank he unleashed violent attacks on Maria and the children. After enduring years of his abuse, she mustered the courage to pack up herself and her children and start again.

Maria described her "new" life as one full of obligations and void of nurturance. "All I did was go to work, come home and cook dinner, help the kids with their homework, and then get them to bed. By the time all that was finished, I had no energy for anything but to sit in front of the television and eat. I had no friends, no one to talk to. The only comfort I could find was in food."

It was ironic that eating, one of the few things Maria did for herself, should also be hazardous to her health. A nurse practitioner at the community clinic warned her that her increasing weight was a danger to her health. But Maria seemed unable to place limits on her eating. "Somehow that pizza, that box of cookies, or that bottle of soda gave me the only pleasure I had in life," Maria recalled. "Of course, I was also obsessed with losing weight. I was always trying one diet or another, whatever caught my eye on the cover of the magazines at the supermarket checkout counter." But rarely was Maria able to stay on a diet longer than two or three days. She did not like the way she looked, which only made her feel less lovable and more susceptible to overeating.

One day at work, Mr. Stevens, Maria's boss, asked if the ten women in the secretarial pool would come in to work an hour earlier and stay a little later while a major audit from the company's home office was being carried out. "I was furious!" Maria recalled angrily. "We had asked the company a few months earlier either for a pay raise to help with child care expenses or for the company to provide a small day care center in the building for employees. The management told us they couldn't afford either option this fiscal year, maybe the next. Then Mr. Stevens had the nerve to ask us to sacrifice even more for the company! And with no assistance offered for the additional child care we would need." Maria knew that complying with this request would mean trying to find someone who could cover all those extra hours. And, of course, it would mean even less time with her children.

Maria admitted, "I wanted to say, 'No way! You are asking too much!' " She smiled sheepishly, "But what I did say was, 'Sure, Mr. Stevens. Of course I'll be there. You know you can always depend on me.' I must have gained an extra fifteen pounds that month, I was so angry."

Maria had fallen prey to the second lie of the Messiah Trap: "Everyone else's needs take priority over mine." While she had been able to stand up to the abuse of her ex-husband, Maria was not yet able to create a life for herself and her children that included the love and nurturance they legitimately needed. Like many codependents caught in the helpaholic lifestyle of the Messiah Trap, Maria's life was characterized by more than one addiction. She was addicted to helping and to eating in self-destructive ways.

"I turned to my church," Maria explained, "hoping I could find some relief there. One Sunday night I was really down on myself. I had been keeping those extra hours at work. The overtime pay did not begin to cover the added child care. I came into the church feeling completely empty, except for a rage at my boss that kept filling my mind. I felt so confused. One minute I was feeling angry, the next feeling guilty for feeling angry, and then angry at feeling guilty. I just went round and round."

Maria fidgeted throughout the service. She stood with the congregation to sing "Dare to be Daniel, Dare to Stand Alone" and "Take My Life and Let It Be." The words in these songs increased her feelings of guilt and inadequacy. Then the pastor read the

Scripture: "It shall not be so among you; but whoever would be great among you must be your servant, and whoever would be first among you must be your slave; even as I came not to be served but to serve, and to give my life as a ransom for many" (Matthew 20:26–28).

The pastor began his sermon. "I want to talk to you tonight about selfishness. Sin is nothing but selfishness. We want our own way, not God's way. We live in a selfish world. The 'me' generation, they call it. Everyone thinks of their own needs first of all.

"Christians should be different. We should not think of our own needs first of all. Jesus is our model. As it said in our Scripture lesson, Jesus came to serve, not to be served. He came to give up his life. That is how we should act."

Maria sat bombarded with conflicting feelings. "What the pastor said sounded right and yet it felt so wrong. But what did that mean? He was the one who had studied God's word for years. Who was I to say he was wrong? I felt that I was letting my kids down by spending so many extra hours at work, but how could I say no to my boss? My children really needed and deserved to be cared for by someone responsible and loving. Was I really being selfish for wanting to spend more time with them? Was it really selfish to want them to have quality child care, instead of the inadequate care of neighborhood teenagers And in the back of my mind came a small voice crying, 'What about me?' "

Maria's head swam while the pastor's voice climbed toward the emotional climax of the sermon. "You must nail your selfishness to the cross. You must be killed if you are to live again. Nail it all to the cross. Your pettiness. Your complaining. Your griping. Right now, who will come forward to this altar and nail their selfishness to the cross of Jesus Christ?"

Maria felt pulled in two directions. She felt guilty and she resented feeling guilty. She stood up to respond, but instead of heading for the altar, Maria quietly walked out of the church. She explained softly, "It was like something in me snapped. I had never resisted an altar call before. I have always wanted to be sensitive to God's leading. But there was something that told me that what I was hearing was not God's voice. No, this was the same voice that had told me not to leave the abuse of my husband, the same voice that kept telling me to eat too much." Maria had begun to recognize the voice of the Messiah Trap.

The voice of the Messiah Trap may sound right, especially when it comes from someone with credentials or in a position of authority. But the Messiah Trap leads only to further bondage, to lower self-esteem, and ultimately to self-destruction. God's voice leads us gently to reconciliation and renewal. The voice of the Messiah Trap is laced with accusations, while God's voice enfolds us in love. Maria struggled to discern between these voices. "I was so confused when I walked out of the sanctuary that night. I kept praying, 'Lord Jesus, more than anything I want to follow you. I know I can be selfish. I pray you will forgive me if I am being selfish now.'" With that, Maria picked up her children in the nursery and drove home. She put her children to bed in silence. Maria recalled, "It was the first time in a long time I didn't feel compelled to eat. I was still very confused, but somehow felt I had made an important and right step."

The Perspective of Scarcity

Without malicious intent, Charles's and Maria's churches were setting the Messiah Trap. We agree with the doctor who spoke to the adult class at Charles's church when she pointed out that we Americans consume far more than our share of the world's resources. And we agree that Jesus teaches us to gain our lives by offering ourselves in loving service to others. We also agree with the pastor when he preached that selfishness is sinful. Jesus does model for us a life of service rather than a life of being served.

However, there is also a form of sin that is not selfishness but excessive selflessness. We can empty ourselves in such a way that we simply destroy ourselves. There is a kind of obsessive action that is not love but unhealthy neglect of our own wholeness.

The crux of the problem lies in the way Scriptures concerning self-denial and self-sacrifice are interpreted. We believe it is a matter of perspective. We can look at these passages (and everything else in the Bible) from the perspective of plenty: there is *more* than enough; or the perspective of scarcity: there is *never* enough. When the church sets the Messiah Trap, both the speaker and the hearer approach Scripture from the perspective of scarcity.

What is the spiritual perspective of scarcity? It is the attitude that God has put an insufficient amount of what we need into the world. Since there is not enough for everyone, what little there is must be carefully rationed, like a small canteen of water in a hot, dry desert. Those who experience life as scarcity do not expect to find water from other sources. They do not know how to locate and tap underground springs. Stumbling past cacti and other desert plants, they suffer thirst rather than learn from these plants that draw nourishment from a seemingly hostile earth.

In the same way, Christians too often assume that there is not enough goodness and self-worth, and especially not enough of God's love, to go around. When caught in the Messiah Trap, we simply do not believe that each of us is of infinite value to God— right now, just as we are, with no additional effort required on our part. Like the wanderer in the desert, we act as if God's love is a canteen of water that must be carefully rationed, offered only to the truly deserving. When we believe God's love is in short supply, we struggle to prove ourselves lovable with the same intensity we would display in fighting for a drop of water from the canteen. Our emotional lives become dry and empty. Our spiritual quest becomes a fight for survival.

The perspective of scarcity is also like a starvation diet. Imagine what it would feel like to be a part of a small band of sailors adrift on a life raft in the middle of the Atlantic Ocean after your boat had sunk. Thousands of miles from land, you and the others have only one chance for survival: to stay alive long enough to be rescued. With only a couple cans of beans, a tin of crackers, and a few liters of water, there is not enough food to go around. You find yourself diverting your eyes, afraid the others will see you longing for the insufficient rations. Trying to shake the guilt, you can't help hoping that some of the others will volunteer to give up their lives and give you their portion. Without meaning to, you naturally start to assess which of the survivors are more "valuable" than the others. Choices of life and death have to be made in such situations of scarcity, and we naturally base our decisions on some sense of personal value or lovableness.

Whether we are literally on a life raft in the middle of the ocean or sitting in the pew of a beautifully decorated church, when we operate from the perspective of scarcity we never extend love and a sense of value to *all* people. The church caught in the Messiah Trap will read the Scriptures, and especially Jesus' teachings about self-sacrifice and self-denial, as if we were slowly dying on a life raft. We will act as if we are on a spiritual starvation diet. In these congregations, there will never be enough of the love of God for everyone. The few crumbs of God's love, the tiny droplets of God's approval, must be carefully rationed.

Ironically, the same congregations that are so stingy with God's love are usually the very ones that demand the most from their members. What little self-esteem each member has is often demanded and taken away. These Christians obey the lies of the Messiah Trap and give up their tiny, inadequate rations. They bow to pressure, sacrificing in such a way that no one is truly loved. The act of giving becomes an empty gesture, a futile exercise, even an act of suicide.

A person caught in the first lie of the Messiah Trap, "If I don't do it, it won't get done," believes, like Charles, that there is not enough to go around. Because of the perceived scarcity, Charles felt compelled to sacrifice his portion. Feeling stronger, more privileged, Charles unconsciously believed that if he didn't rescue the others by depriving himself, then all would be lost.

A person caught in the second lie of the Messiah Trap, "Everyone else's needs take priority over mine," also believes there is not enough for everyone involved. Convinced of her own unworthiness, Maria felt undeserving of what little she had. As a codependent, she allowed the needs of others to take complete priority over her own, even when it meant she was being destroyed as a person and her family was being deprived. Maria gave all she had, not out of love, but out of the despair of feeling unloved by God.

It is tragically destructive to view life from the perspective of the spiritual life raft, from the perspective of scarcity. The good news is that this *is not* Jesus' perspective and *need not* be ours. We believe that all of Jesus' teaching, especially his teaching about self-sacrifice, comes from the perspective of plenty. The meal of plenty is a common image in Jesus' teaching. While on earth, he lived out this joyous and nourishing perspective as he ate with tax collectors, sinners, and women—people who had been rejected by others. There was plenty of God's love and forgiveness for everyone. Jesus turned no one away.

We believe that the perspective of scarcity is rooted in a misunderstanding of who God is and of how God loves us. Biblical teachings about self-sacrifice mistakenly coupled with the perspective of scarcity add up to a dangerous combination. It pushes people like Charles and Maria into futile, helpaholic ways of living. The solution comes in changing our perspective and daring to believe that there is enough to go around. In God, all thirst can be quenched, all the hungry can be fed. Jesus spoke of living water that leaves us forever satisfied. This abundant water flows on dry ground, making a garden out of our desert. Jesus likens the presence of God to a great banquet with plenty of food for all. This is the promise of God's love that we will explore in later chapters of this book. It is only by understanding and experiencing God's love that we can abandon the perspective of scarcity. But if we and our churches have fallen into the Messiah Trap, it is critical that we recognize that the perspective of scarcity itself is based on distorted images of God. We must see these images for the idols they are and overcome them.

CHAPTER 4

Is Your God an
Absent Parent?

How long, O Lord? Will you forget me forever?
  How long will you hide your face from me?
How long must I bear pain in my soul,
  and have sorrow in my heart all the day?
—Psalm 13:1–2

"Why Heidi?" Cheryl asked Robert. "She was such a good Christian girl. She never took drugs or got into trouble. It doesn't make sense that she should get cancer and die."

In the days since Heidi's funeral, Cheryl had grown more, not less, confused. Robert, a cousin of Cheryl's who lived in town, had heard she was taking Heidi's death pretty hard. He had made a special effort to clear out some time in his otherwise hectic schedule as the administrator of a shelter caring for runaways and teenage prostitutes. Robert had invited Cheryl out to lunch, hoping to cheer her up. But their conversation had quickly turned from catching up on family news to Heidi. Cheryl and Robert had always been close, even though Robert was rather proud of his role as the family atheist.

"I did everything I could," Cheryl said. "I visited her in the hospital every day. Her parents needed help with the medical bills, so I organized a special fundraising effort in the community. But the other day, several of Heidi's friends cornered me, all sobbing. They thought I should have all the answers. After all, I am a minister. I didn't know what to say. I feel so helpless. How could God let this happen?"

"God?" Robert scoffed. "What does God have to do with anything?" Robert was the kind of man who dived in head first and then asked the depth of the water. He was usually the first to arrive and the last to leave, with shirt sleeves rolled up to the elbow and a serious, but deeply compassionate, glint in his eye. His huge hands could curl into fists and match any assailant or gently curl around a sleeping baby.

"Where is God when all the suffering is going on?" Robert asked Cheryl. "Why didn't God help Heidi? Anytime God wants to show up and make a difference, I won't stand in the way. In the meantime, I've got too many people who need help to sit around in some church thanking a God who hasn't come through."

In his work with those who called the streets their home, he had seen children die in poverty, young women age before their time, and the pride of young men crushed by the hopelessness of the streets. Robert had seen it all, so he said, and as he searched the faces of the lost, hungry wanderers, he claimed he never once saw the face of God.

"What I see," he said angrily, "are faces filled with confusion and misery. When I first moved to this city, I was struck by the beauty of the architecture and the skyline. I've become blind to all that now. Now all I see is the pain."

Leaning back from the table with a smug look on his face, Robert said, "You ask me how God fits into all of this? Well, I figure it this way. If God were all-good, then God would want to do something about evil and suffering. God would have wanted to prevent Heidi's death. And if God were all-powerful, then God would be capable of doing something about this mess. God would have been able to keep Heidi alive." Swinging his arm to point out the window, he exclaimed, "But take a look! This world is full to the brim with injustice and cruelty. Evil is everywhere. Your Heidi died, even though she was a 'good Christian girl.' So either God isn't all that good or all that powerful. Or maybe," Robert paused, sat up, and looked straight at Cheryl, "you could conclude that God isn't good, isn't powerful, and really isn't anything or anyone at all."

The Messiah Trap and the Problem of Evil

What theologians and philosophers call "the problem of evil" confronts all of us who try to help others in any serious way. In fact, the more seriously we take the world in which we live, the more violence, fear, anger, and hopelessness we will encounter. The problem of evil is more than a theoretical puzzle to be discussed over tea; it is a practical crisis for those who hold the hands of young people dying from AIDS, who listen to the sobbed horrors of rape, and who prepare for the memorial services of children who died at the hands of abusive caretakers. These people see evil in human faces and hands and blood and tears.

Evil is easy to spot. It heralds us through the grimy hand that grabs at us and the cracking voice that begs us for a dime. It blurs our vision and clogs our lungs like the smog and pollution that hang over our cities. And if we happen to miss out on our firsthand dose of evil for the day, we can have it served up in tidy thirty-minute packages through the evening news. Like Robert, we may develop eyes well trained to spot the pain but unable to focus on the hope. When we are caught in the Messiah Trap, we try more and more but see less and less success.

Many in our society are too overwhelmed by evil and suffering to be able to believe that God is present in the world. "Quite frankly," Robert said to Cheryl, "I just don't see God doing anything, and there's too much to do to sit around talking about an ineffectual God. So, to answer your question, I guess I have to say that God doesn't fit in anywhere. As I see it, it's really up to me to make a difference and it's worth any sacrifice I have to make."

It is easy for the atheist to fall into the Messiah Trap. Robert, and those who believe similarly, live life as if they are totally responsible and completely alone. With no higher power in which to trust, the atheist truly is the only one available to care and to help. This is the first lie of the Messiah Trap: "If I don't do it, it won't get done." Then, when a person like Robert confronts the enormity of the need in our troubled world, it is quite natural to conclude that there is no time to rest and no time to lose. This pushes him or her into the second lie of the Messiah Trap: "Everyone else's needs take priority over mine."

Cheryl disagreed with Robert's conclusions and asserted that God does, in fact, exist and responds actively to this world's sufferings. As do many Christians who have fallen into the Messiah Trap, however, she had more in common with Robert than she realized. While the problem of evil pushes some, like Robert, into embracing theoretical atheism, it leads Cheryl, and others like her, to live out a practical atheism. Cheryl said she believed in God, but she acted as if the whole world depended upon her.

Oddly enough, this practical atheism is really a form of idolatry. We usually think of idolatry as the worship of a stone or wooden image of God. But anything that we care deeply about or depend upon can become an idol: an idea, a cause, a person, or an institution. Even the images or concepts of God we develop from our experiences can become idols. Christians may fall into the Messiah Trap because their images of God are distorted or idolatrous. These idolatrous images of God have little to do with the God of love Jesus proclaims. Instead, they are constructed out of our all-too-human uses and abuses of power.

It is true that our human images of God always fall short of the reality toward which they point. But it is just as true that our human images of God are the lenses through which we normally experience God. An idolatrous or distorted image of God may keep good, committed people from experiencing God's love and may lead them to the practical atheism of the Messiah Trap. Two specific, distorted, idolatrous images of God may lead to the Messiah Trap: God the Absent Parent and God the Abusive Parent.

God the Absent Parent

"But Robert," Cheryl insisted emphatically, "God is at the center of all I do! I make sure the youth group is well grounded in solid Bible study. I am very proud of my religious heritage." She paused and smiled at herself. "I sound like the church's informational brochure." Then her face grew serious. "To be honest with you, though, I don't know where God fits in anymore. I used to, but now, well, when I pray, when I try to pray about Heidi's death, I feel helpless and frustrated, like a small child."

Cheryl's eyes darkened as she remembered her childhood. "As you know, my dad left us when I was eight," she recalled. "I came home from school one day and he was gone. Mom was at the kitchen table crying. I was confused and frightened, so I asked her what was wrong. She said angrily, 'He's left us. Just like a man to desert us like this. You can never trust them.' I tried to ask where he went, but she stopped me. 'We're never going to talk about that man again. We'll show him that we don't need him. We don't need anyone. . . .'

"So I learned to live without him," Cheryl sighed. "We never spoke his name again. Mom went to work, and my brother and I did odd jobs after school. Somehow we got by. Sometimes I wish I could talk with Dad about problems I'm having or just be with him. But I don't know, after all these years, if I'd even recognize him if I saw him on the street."

Cheryl's sadness turned to anger. "Why did he leave me like that! He left me without a word, no phone call, not one birthday present. Christmas after Christmas I begged God to bring him back to me. I would make a deal with God each year that I would give away all my presents to other needy children if God would only bring my father back on Christmas Eve." Cheryl's warm, green eyes filled with tears. "Each Christmas morning I would run downstairs hoping that this year God would answer my prayer, only to be let down. I don't think my mother ever understood why I was so sad as I opened my Christmas presents. Times were hard for us financially, without Dad, and she tried to make up for his absence by buying nice gifts. To me, though, the presents reminded me that I couldn't depend on my father."

"It sounds to me like you are beginning to have the same feelings toward God," Robert said gently, without his usual sarcasm.

Cheryl took a breath as if to protest, paused, and then slumped back into her chair. "I hate to admit that. I really do. If I were a good Christian, I would trust God more. I pray and ask God to bless my ministry, but deep down I don't expect any real assistance. I couldn't count on God to bring my Dad back to me on Christmas Eve. What makes me think I can expect anything from God now?"

Cheryl's dilemma is a common one, especially for those who have felt neglected and let down by their parents. Where is God when we are in need? Can we count on real help with real crises, or do we give lip service to a God up there somewhere in the sky and then face alone the numerous problems that beset us? Many people who claim to be ministering in the name of God actually deny God's power or relevance on a practical basis in their daily routines. They view God as an Absent Parent, inaccessible to the children who need an attentive and loving response. This distorted view of God is often created out of human experiences of being abandoned by those we should have been able to trust.

It is easy to see how Cheryl correlated her earthly father with God. She craved intimacy with her father and experienced only disappointment. The loss of a parent through divorce is not the only way a child can be set up for this distorted image of God. Many people from intact families also experience an absent parent through a variety of factors, such as the illness of a parent, work pressures placed on a parent, or the emotional distance resulting from a parent's inability to be intimate. In these cases, a person's image of God may resemble the aloof executive, minister, or professor whose unresolved issues of control and vulnerability make intimacy nearly impossible. Such parents are incapable of attending to their children and are present only in the brooding, impatient silence of a face hidden behind a newspaper or a book.

Cheryl's God did too little. She expected God to keep good teenagers like Heidi from getting sick or to intervene powerfully when they did. When God didn't act the way she expected, Cheryl began to experience God as absent, just as her own father had been. The evil and suffering surrounding Heidi's death caused Cheryl to doubt God's presence in the world. This, in turn, led her to feel alone and totally responsible for doing something about Heidi's illness and death. Cheryl began to torture herself with frantic activity, guilt, and self-doubt. God was not a source of help, for in Cheryl's distorted image of God, God was an Absent Parent.

Christians who mistakenly view God as an Absent Parent easily fall prey to the Messiah Trap. These dedicated people understand their work to be divinely authorized. But because God does not seem to do anything about the death of young people, the abuse of children, the poverty of the elderly, or any of the other obvious evils in the world, these caring people begin to act as if *they* were God, as if it were by *their* goodness and power that all the evil in the world had to be removed. For those who experience God as an Absent Parent, the first lie of the Messiah Trap, "If I don't do it, it won't get done," comes to mean, "God doesn't seem to be doing anything about evil, so I must do it." We begin to confuse our roles as representatives of God with *being God.* We take up the role God seems to have vacated.

But we are not God. None of us has the goodness or power to eliminate all the evil we encounter. None of us can carry the load of the world. When we try, we are crushed, as Cheryl was. When a human being seeks to take God's place in the world, even if for the best of reasons, that person will not only fail to be God but will also be destroyed as a human being. The end result of our counterfeit messiahship, like that of Jesus' authentic messiahship, is crucifixion. Our self-crucifixions, however, are not redemptive, just tragic.

CHAPTER 5

Is Your God
an Abusive Parent?

How then can I dispute with God?
How can I find words to argue with God?
Even if I summoned God and God responded,
I do not believe I would be given a hearing.
God would crush me with a storm
and multiply my wounds for no reason.
God would not let me regain my breath
but would overwhelm me with misery.
—Job 9:14, 16–18 (NIV)

If there were ever two people who claimed to trust God, it was Sid and Ronda, an energetic couple who came for marital counseling. In the struggle to save their tenuous marriage, Sid repeatedly referred to his faith in God. "I believe that God is in control of this world and has a plan for Ronda and me. Divorce is not part of God's will. We've got to work this out somehow. God will help us." Sid's words served as both encouragement and irritation for Ronda, who felt supported by her own faith but bruised by Sid. "I agree that God will help us," Ronda responded to Sid's declaration, "but how can you say that God's in control of everything? You aren't blaming God for the mess we're in, are you?"

"Of course not!" Sid seemed distressed. "I'm not blaming God for anything!"

Ronda looked at the marriage counselor and raised her hands in despair. "This is the kind of logic I have had to put up with all our married lives." Looking back at her husband, she insisted, "Sid, if God is *totally* in control of this world, then God is responsible for the bad as well as the good. God is to blame for our troubled marriage."

The room was silent as all pondered the dilemma. Ronda broke the silence. "I was just spouting off in anger at Sid, but I have to admit that a part of me really is angry at God. I have always believed that God created this world and is in control of its destiny. That's what I was taught as a little girl in Sunday school. So why haven't our lives turned out the way they were supposed to? Why hasn't God healed our marriage?"

God the Abusive Parent

Ronda and Sid were caught in a maze of twisted thinking that originates in the distorted view of a God who does "too much." In this line of thinking, God is responsible directly or indirectly for everything that happens in the world, including all the broken promises, broken relationships, and broken hearts. What begins as an attempt to honor God as all-powerful soon deteriorates into an image of a God who could put an end to evil but won't, or who even takes sadistic delight in our suffering. It is impossible to trust or be loyal to a God whose actions destroy and cause pain to others.

Ronda began to weep. "I've never allowed myself to say I was angry at God before. It scares me so much. What if God punishes me?"

To understand where such a fear of God might originate, the counselor asked Ronda to talk about her family when she was growing up. Ronda explained that she had been the youngest child in a large, loud, and chaotic family where survival meant staying out of her father's way. He ruled his family with an erratic, iron hand that made it difficult to know what to expect. "I tried to please him," Ronda confessed, "but I never could tell what he wanted. Some days he would love for me to run up and hug him when he came home, and other days he would push me away." She rubbed her arms as if caressing a bruise. "He never knew his own strength. I'm sure he never meant to hurt me."

Like Ronda, children who are raised by abusive, demanding parents are susceptible to a distorted image of God as abusive and demanding. But admitting that one views God in such a way is quite painful and often just too frightening. So, like the child trying to please an abusive parent, the Christian tries to do the impossible: appease this demanding authority figure through sacrifice and suffering. A person who believes that God is abusive is set up for the second lie of the Messiah Trap: "Everyone else's needs take priority over mine."

People who share this view of God come from all kinds of backgrounds and all walks of life. However, they do have one thing in common. Like Sid and Ronda, they are always looking for someone to *blame*. These Messiahs do not feel safe, do not feel worthy, do not feel loved. In an attempt to earn the love of God, they try to be perfect. When things do go wrong, they assume someone was at fault. For those who mistakenly view God as an Abusive Parent, suffering and evil occur because someone has sinned and God is punishing the guilty party. The sin and the sinner must be uncovered. The person to blame must be found out.

Sharing the view of God as an Abusive Parent, Sid tried to respond to his wife's fears. "I don't think God will punish you if you repent. In fact, God could save this marriage if we would confess the sin in our lives. God has promised to bless those homes that follow the guidelines set forth in Scripture." Sid folded his arms confidently, as if he had found the solution.

Ronda began to bristle. "I know exactly what you're trying to say, Sid, with all that pious talk. You're trying to blame me for our problems, that somehow I've not been a godly wife, that somehow I have sinned." Angry tears continued to spill down her face. "After all the times you have harassed me, bullied me, and hurt my feelings, I can't believe you have the nerve to blame me for our problems!"

"Well, you've been trying to place the blame on me and God!" Sid shot back. "I've done everything I can to make you happy, tried to protect you from the harsh outside world, and this is the thanks I get!"

Sid and Ronda were uncovering one of the most fundamental human issues: control. Sin can be understood as an inappropriate settling of the issue of control. Our sinful tendency is to act as if God expects us to do something to win God's approval. When we fall into the Messiah Trap, this is often translated into the demand that we do something *for* someone else. Some Christians caught in the Messiah Trap try to solve all problems (and try to win God's approval) by taking control. We often hanker to make our children, friends, and spouses "shape up." Sid wanted to save his marriage and felt that the way to do it was by controlling his wife. In so doing, he was mimicking the way he felt God, as an Abusive Parent, acts toward people. Christians who view God as abusive often feel it is not only their right but their obligation to control others. Of course, we don't admit that we are trying to control others. We prefer to say that we are trying to help others.

But there is another way of settling the issue of control. In every abusive situation there is both an abuser and an abused victim. Like the abuser, the victim believes he or she must *do* something to gain a sense of self-worth. The abused person, however, does not control others, but becomes inappropriately dependent and allows another person to control them to such an extent that their freedom and value as a person is lost. Ronda had tried desperately to please first her father and then Sid, even though it meant continual sacrifice of her own legitimate needs. In so doing, she was mimicking the way she felt she ought to act toward God as an Abusive Parent. Christians who view God as abusive often feel they have no value and that their suffering is justified punishment for their misdeeds.

In the final analysis, this strategy is a form of idolatry, for we are demanding that the meaning of our lives must be the product of our own effort. The problem with idolatry is simple: the idol cannot bear the weight. We cannot succeed in bringing all of life under our own control. Other people will resist our attempts, even when we feel our efforts are "for their own good," for they are persons with their own intrinsic value, not just objects for our power or good intentions. We cannot be whole persons if we are inappropriately dependent on another person. Sooner or later we will come to resent the control others exert over us.

Ronda's face grew dark and rigid. "Sid, I will never thank you for pushing me around. Do you understand that?"

"All I know," Sid shot back with hatred in his eyes, "is that I have been a good husband to you. I have followed God to the best of my ability. If there is any problem in our marriage, it is not on my part. You are the one who has never learned how to submit properly to her husband!"

As Ronda resisted Sid's attempts to control her, the battle escalated. People who view God as abusive are often blind to the abuse they perpetrate on others. Like Sid, they often justify their abusive behavior as being godlike. And, in fact, it is, for if one worships the idolatrous image of God as an Abusive Parent, one will likely become abusive as well.

Because she believed that God sent evil and suffering into her life to punish her, Ronda lost all sense of her own worth as a person. For her, the second lie of the Messiah Trap, "Everyone else's needs take priority over mine" had come to mean "Because God does not respect my value as a person, it doesn't matter if other people mistreat me too."

When we are caught in the Messiah Trap, we know only how to relate to others through control or inappropriate dependence. The resistance of those we try to control will threaten us. And so we are forced to exert even more control over them. When our value as persons is abused by others we become angry and strike back, desperate for independence. This spiral of physical, psychological, and spiritual violence can grow, slowly destroying both the abuser and the victim. Ronda and Sid were tearing down their marriage through this destructive cycle, all in the name of God. But where do you turn when the God you serve is infinitely cruel? Where do you run for safety when the God who sees all delights in your pain? When caught in the Messiah Trap, the image of God as an Abusive Parent is part of the problem, not the solution, and, like quicksand, it leaves the struggling victim sinking deeper into despair.

Messiah Trap Theology

Jenny, Cheryl, Charles, Maria, and Ronda all have something in common: God has no positive, practical impact in their lives. If there is any impact at all, it is negative. For these Christians caught in the Messiah Trap, God is either absent (unhearing, uncaring, and useless) or abusive (demanding, perfectionistic, and cruel). At best, they have been left to fend for themselves, or, at worst, enslaved to sacrifice themselves and others to a sadist who is impossible to please. Each person's story is different, but the underlying issues are the same: power and control, powerlessness and lack of self-worth.

Jenny, Cheryl, Charles, Maria, and Ronda all assume that true power is coercive, the ability to control another person, to make another person do what we want them to do. This view of power comes from our dealings with things. We do control and coerce inanimate objects: coffee cups, nails, keyboards, and so on. We usually do not consider the intrinsic value of such objects. Unfortunately, we too often relate to ourselves and other people in just this depersonalized way.

The foundation of Messiah Trap theology, the idolatrous images of God as Absent or Abusive Parent, is laid when we transfer this view of coercive power to God. The tendency is common. Think of our usual views of God's attributes: eternal, immutable, omnipotent. Don't we tend to view God as totally independent of us and completely self-sufficient? Hasn't God been described as completely unchanged by anything that happens to us for good or for ill? Don't many of us think of God as able to do literally anything God wants to do without consideration for any other individual?

Such a view assumes that God's purposes are purely self-contained; that God has no regard for others when God acts. Such a view of God can be a compensating strategy for our own sense of powerlessness. The two idolatrous images can be unconscious attempts on our part to take control. There is security in the thought that God does all. But then life, with its evil and suffering, comes along, bringing disappointment. Either God the Absent Parent seemingly fails to exercise the unlimited, coercive power we wish God would exert (this sets up side one of the Messiah Trap: "If I don't do it, it won't get done"), or the coercive power of God the Abusive Parent seems to be exercised to harm and not to help (setting up the second side of the Messiah Trap: "Everyone else's needs take priority over mine"). But all this is idolatry. In these views we have deformed God into the image of our own sinful uses and abuses of power.

If lives like those of Jenny, Cheryl, Charles, Maria, and Ronda are to be transformed, a more adequate image of God must be discovered. An image of God as attentive and nurturing love must shatter the idols of God as Absent Parent and Abusive Parent. We must really believe, practically not just theoretically, that God is love and that the true power of God lies not in coercing us but in taking our suffering and sin into God's own life and redeeming it. If Christians caught in the Messiah Trap can experience God as loving them unconditionally, then they may begin to escape the lies and accept themselves and others in love. Then, and only then, will their actions toward others flow from a sense of their own worth and of the worth of those whom they serve.

The Spiral of Service

CHAPTER **6**

What Is Love?

Love is patient and kind; love is not jealous or
boastful; it is not arrogant or rude. Love does not
insist on its own way; it is not irritable or resentful;
it does not rejoice at wrong, but rejoices in the
right. Love bears all things, believes all things,
hopes all things, endures all things.
—1 Corinthians 13:4–7

Marjorie stared in amazement as Charles, her brother-in-law, reached over to squeeze her sister Sara's hand. Unaware that he was being watched, Charles smiled affectionately into his wife's eyes. Charles, Sara, and their two children had recently returned from a year in Argentina where Charles had taught and conducted research at the national university. Marjorie had invited Charles and Sara over to share slides and stories of their time abroad with family and friends. As brightly colored slides of Buenos Aires flashed on the living room wall and Charles continued his entertaining narrative for the others, Marjorie quietly pulled Sara into the kitchen.

"What has happened to Charles?" Marjorie whispered. "I've never seen him so warm toward you, so . . . . "

"So comfortable?" Sara suggested.

"Yes, that's it. What happened to all of you down there? He was so tense and overextended before you left."

Sara's face glowed with a deep and contented smile. "It's quite simple, Marjorie. Charles discovered love."

Marjorie looked through the doorway at her brother-in-law with one hand naturally cupped atop his daughter's head and the other clicking slide after slide. "Love?" she echoed, as if it were a foreign word Sara had picked up in her travels. Pulling her sister down into a chair next to her and looking Sara straight in the eye, Marjorie asked sincerely, "Love? Uh, could you be more specific?"

Marjorie is not alone. For many, *love* has lost its meaning. The word has been trivialized by its overuse in our culture. Advertisers tell us to love our cars, our carpets, our carpet cleaners, and our coffee makers (especially with their digital command centers). With so many things to love, so many gadgets, it becomes hard to tell another person we love them and mean something more by it than finding them a pleasant diversion in our busy lives.

It is also difficult to speak of love in our culture without immediately thinking of sex. Don't we hesitate sometimes to say we love someone because we are afraid it will imply a sexual agenda that may not be part of the relationship? Isn't this hesitancy particularly strong among men, even very close friends, who can't say "I love you" because of the culturally ingrained fear of homosexuality?

In the dictionary of late twentieth century American culture— the culture of television, *People* magazine, and shopping malls— the usual definition of love runs something like this:

> love (luv) 1. *the warm emotion or state of feeling in which a person is attracted to a thing or person they find desirable;* 2. *a relationship based on sexual feelings or interests.*

As long as this is what we understand love to mean, we will have difficulty developing an image of God as love that can overcome the idolatrous images of God as Absent Parent and Abusive Parent. First, love itself must be redefined.

A New Image of Love

One strand of modern theology argues against the popular views of love as a state of feeling and as sexual attraction. This strand can be traced back to Anders Nygren's classic book *Agape and Eros* (translated by Philip Watson, revised edition, London: S.P.C.K., 1953). Nygren said that love is not a state of feeling but a state of being, a way in which persons exist in relation to others. Nygren's main point was that there are two different forms of love: *eros* and *agape*. It is the *agape* form of love that characterizes Christianity.

Nygren described the contrast between *eros* and *agape* in the following way. *Eros* is acquisitive desire; *agape* is sacrificial giving. *Eros* is an upward movement from human beings to God. *Agape* moves downward from God to human beings. *Eros* is our human effort; *agape* is God's grace. *Eros* is egocentric, a noble form of self-assertion; *agape* is unselfish and gives itself away. *Eros* seeks to gain its life; *agape* dares to lose its life. *Eros* is determined by the beauty and worth of its object; it is not spontaneous but evoked and motivated. *Agape* is self-sufficient in relation to its object; it is spontaneous, overflowing, and unmotivated. *Eros* recognizes its object as valuable and then loves it. *Agape* loves and then creates value in its object.

Nygren's view of the two forms of love sparked a lively debate. (For information see the "Further Reading" section at the end of this book.) Many theologians and ethicists have tried to present a more balanced understanding of the importance and interrelationship of *eros* and *agape*. They say that both forms of love are good in themselves and should not be separated in Christian thought and life. But most agreed with Nygren's view that *eros* and *agape* are the two basic forms of love and that *agape* is defined by self-sacrifice.

In the last twenty years, however, this basic agreement with Nygren has been challenged in two ways. First, a number of thinkers have attempted a better analysis of the one spirit or nature of love that is present in all the forms of love. Their conclusion is that self-sacrifice is just one aspect of genuine love. Actively giving of oneself to another person must be preceded by a receiving of the other person into one's life. Second, a number of other theologians have argued that Nygren's view of Christian love as self-sacrifice is one-sided and that in a sexist culture it reinforces the mistaken view that women should sacrifice their personhood for that of the men to whom they are related, although the men do not make a corresponding self-sacrifice. Instead, these thinkers believe that love is mutuality, with giving and receiving by both partners.

Both groups criticize the idea that love is nothing but sacrificial self-giving. We believe that these recent discussions provide the basis for a better understanding of love. We offer the following as a working definition of love:

> *To love is to allow another person to make a real difference in one's life, and, because of the difference the other person makes, to act toward the other person so as to assist her or him to develop fully as a person.*

Our definition will be clearer if we personalize it by putting in names of two people, let's say Charles and Sara. For Charles, love means allowing Sara to make a real difference in his life and, because of the difference Sara makes, acting toward her so as to assist her to develop more fully as a person. Likewise, if Sara loves Charles, she will allow him to make a real difference in her life, and, because of the difference he makes in her life, Sara will act toward Charles so as to assist him to develop fully as a person.

This means that love does not have just one side, one characteristic, that of self-sacrifical action, but two: (1) *receptivity* or openness to the other person and (2) self-giving *activity*. In real life, the two sides of love cannot be separated. There is no genuine love without both receptivity and activity. However, they can and should be discussed one at a time.

The Receptivity of Love

When we love, we are first of all vulnerable to another person as we open ourselves to them. We allow them to make a difference in our lives so that we are no longer the same people we were before we loved. This means we allow the other person's life to become a part of our lives. Their interests, feelings, likes, dislikes, plans, and wishes become included within our interests, feelings, likes, dislikes, plans, and wishes. In this first side of love, we receive another person into ourself.

If we love someone, we allow them to claim our attention, affection, and action. Who we are is affected, changed, redefined by the life of the person we love. This should not be confused with an unhealthy dependence on another person in which one's identity is smothered by or based on the other person. Our interests and feelings are enriched, not replaced, by the other person's. If we love someone, we include their plans and wishes within our own life, but their lives should not dominate our own.

Many of us resist allowing another person to affect us deeply. Our culture values independence and self-reliance over vulnerability and mutuality. Charles learned, as a young boy, to stand back from others, to protect his heart with a shield of competence. It was important to Charles to act as if he were in control of his life. He found it very difficult to allow other people to help him or to be involved with his deepest needs. His attitude in life was typical of many Messiahs: "Because I am more competent than most of the people around me, if I want things done right, I ought to do them myself."

Charles was the oldest child in a family of two boys and two girls. A model child, Charles was serious, studious, and obedient. When Charles was ten, his younger sister was born. Almost immediately, the baby faced life-threatening health problems. Charles, his brother, and other sister spent hours in the lobby of the hospital waiting for their parents to come down from the intensive care unit. As his parents spent many long days and nights at the hospital, ten-year-old Charles became an adult. He kept his own tears in check by wiping those of his younger brother and sister. His own fears were contained by battling those of his siblings. Sitting on a chair in the hospital, Charles became the third parent in the family.

Charles's sister pulled through and the family settled down to a normal, happy, stable routine. But Charles had lost his childhood, having been too soon ushered into a world of adult responsibilities. It was not his parents' fault. Charles took the responsibilities upon himself. But the experience shaped his life.

As an adult, Charles had trouble sharing responsibility. He preferred to work alone. While he got along with others and was well liked, it was much easier for him to put in a whole weekend of work on a project by himself than to ask someone else for assistance. Even when Charles did share the work, he often revised the other person's work to meet his own criteria.

Sara recalled how Charles behaved in those days. "He was so closed off from all of us, as if he had built a wall of protection that kept everyone at a safe distance."

Marjorie poured them both a cup of coffee and nodded. "That's exactly how I remember Charles. He was always friendly, but sort of superficial." Thinking back, she continued, "It was as if he lived in his own self-contained world and did not allow other people's lives to penetrate very deeply into his own."

Sara agreed. "Do you remember how much he hated birthdays and Christmas? He never knew what to buy anyone, so he would stall and delay until I ended up buying all the gifts. He would just sign his name on the card. He never took the time to get to know any of us, not even his own children."

"Well, he may have depended on you to buy his gifts, but to the rest of us," Marjorie explained, "Charles was the model of a man in control of his destiny. My husband always felt intimidated by him."

Outwardly, Charles did seem very much in control. Inwardly, however, he felt painfully fragile. The stress of always being in control, always being the responsible person at work, at home, and at social gatherings, exacted a great toll. Charles was wound tight, tight as a violin string about to snap.

Charles claimed to love his wife and children, but in light of the definition of love offered earlier, it is clear that he was not genuinely loving them. While he played the part of the faithful husband and providing father, he was, in fact, absent from his family.

The absent parent represents the opposite of love, whether the parent is physically absent as was Cheryl's father or emotionally absent as was Charles. Instead of allowing spouse and children to make a real difference in their life, the absent parent has an attitude of indifference. And when we are indifferent to another person, we fail to love. We cannot love when we let no one in, for we do not allow their interests, feelings, likes, dislikes, plans, and wishes to claim us or change us or make a difference to us. The opposite of the receptivity of love is to remain utterly unchanged and unmoved by the people around us.

Love simply does not exist unless the life of the other person has made some claim on us. Like Charles, we may fool ourselves into thinking we love other people by merely giving them what we think they need. But unless we allow them into our lives, we cannot know them or know what they really need in life. Any action of ours not called forth by a recognition of their intrinsic value could only be self-imposition, not love.

The Activity of Love

In the first side of love, we accept the other person into our own life, interests, and feelings. We recognize them as valuable. Because of our regard for them as valuable persons, we seek in everything we do toward them to assist their growth as a person.

The second side of love is inseparable from the first and follows it as a response to the other person who has been received into our life. Because the other person makes a difference to us and has made a claim on us, we act toward that person in order to make a difference in their life. We act in every appropriate way to help those we love become more fully and richly themselves. We do not act to further ourselves through those we love, but to further their personhood.

This second side of love is the active one. If we love someone, we are active in caring for them, in seeking to make their life richer. We give of our time, energy, and talent to help the one we love in whatever interests and excites them. In this side of love, our lives become of service to the one we love. It is critical that we recognize, however, that our activity follows from our being receptive. First, we receive the other person into our life. Then and only then can we offer our life as a gift to be received by the other person. In this context, the traditional language of self-sacrifice, of a love that seeks not its own, makes sense. We are free to give of our life, time, and talents to the person we love.

This should not be misunderstood as masochism. It is not that we give ourselves to be used or abused by another person. Rather, we give to the other person because of the wonderful difference they make to us. Our service is not extorted; we offer it freely. Our value as persons is not diminished, it is celebrated. Our service, our effort on behalf of the person we love responds to the value they find in us and we find in them.

Sara grimaced as she sipped her coffee. "I'll tell you what really bothered me about those days. Charles used to guard his time jealously, even selfishly. He found time to take on new projects at the university or at the church. And, of course, he always found the time to play softball in the summer and basketball in the winter. But when I would ask him to clean house or watch the children while I took an evening course at the community college, Charles would complain about not having enough time in his busy schedule. He had trouble supporting my efforts to finish my degree; he even resorted to sabotage. Although he would promise to watch the kids, Charles would often come home late, making me miss my class. I was furious. I resented the double standard."

Marjorie smiled. "Yes, I remember those arguments. You had one in my living room a few years back."

Sara nodded. "Well, we tried to hide our problems from all of you, but sometimes I couldn't keep a lid on my anger! He acted as if his life was more important than ours. It really hurt the children. He treated us like thieves who were stealing his time, rather than human beings he loved."

When we operate from the perspective of scarcity, we act as if it is not possible for everyone to have the space, time, and nurturing they need. Instead of caring for those closest to us, we begin to compete with them, as if we were adrift on the life raft fighting for survival. When Charles saw his wife developing, he unconsciously felt that she was taking something away from him. Her growth threatened him. Although he never would have admitted it, he actually tried to damage Sara rather than build her up. When genuine love is absent, we may become abusive.

As abusers, we adopt an attitude of fear and hatred. We see the time we give as time taken from our own growth. Instead of acting to help the other person become more fully themselves, we come to resent them. Consciously or unconsciously, we try to limit or diminish their development. Like Charles, we view ourselves as more important than those we claim to love.

The Risk of Love

Charles tried to bolster his fragile psyche by dominating Sara and his children. But exerting power over others never really improves anything. Doesn't experience teach that the problem boy in the third grade classroom—the one who acts up, talks back, and fights constantly—does not respond to harsher discipline or more punishment but improves his behavior only when he feels loved by someone? Isn't it true that the woman who has drawn into herself in response to the way others have hurt and taken advantage of her will open up only in a relationship of trust, one in which she is allowed to be herself, without any games of sex and power? Isn't it true that all good friendships and marriages grow out of relationships of mutuality in which *both* persons are affirmed and supported? And aren't we beginning to discover that nations can live together in peace only through mutual trust and vulnerability, not through suspicion and ever-increasing stockpiles of weapons?

Charles may have manipulated Sara into submission, but the seeds of resentment, anger, and rebellion were sown deep. Only love, which begins with acceptance of the beloved, can finally tear down such barriers. Only when people are accepted unconditionally by others and dare to open themselves can they break out of destructive and addictive behaviors.

Marjorie leaned forward. "I know how he used to be, Sara. What I want to know is how this man changed. What happened to all of you in Argentina?"

The breakthrough in Charles's life occurred when he discovered the importance of the two-sided nature of love and was able to risk loving in this double sense. This discovery came about in a most unexpected way.

Charles landed a prestigious and highly competitive research and teaching grant to spend a year at the national university in Argentina. He and his family were very excited about the opportunity. Sara explained, "We talked about the move and decided it would be easier for the children if Charles flew down first and found us a place to live. He had the name of a woman from whom another professor had rented an apartment several years earlier. Charles seemed quite confident in his ability to go to a new country by himself. It never occurred to me that he might be frightened. As usual, he seemed to be in complete control."

In fact, Charles was quite intimidated by having to get along in a foreign culture. Unable to reveal such vulnerability to his wife, however, he put on the face of competence he had learned many years earlier while sitting in the hospital waiting for word about his baby sister.

Even his worst fears fell short of what Charles experienced when he arrived in Buenos Aires. He landed in the middle of the biggest festival of the year. The city was packed with tourists. Virtually no hotel rooms were available. After he found a tiny, overpriced room, Charles called his one contact in Argentina. The woman said her apartment was rented and would be for the entire year. A dead end.

Charles was shocked by how much the language and culture difference affected him. Although he spoke Spanish well for an American, he was extremely self-conscious about his limitations with the language. At home, Charles lived in a world of words. He survived through his adept use of language. Words gave him a sense of power and control. Now, for the first time in his life, his power over words and over himself was gone. He was overwhelmed with feelings of powerlessness. Instead of a strong, capable man, Charles became a small boy, alone and frightened in a world that made no sense.

"I got this phone call in the middle of the night," Sara said. "I could hardly recognize Charles's voice. He was actually sobbing over the phone. A lot of what he said didn't make much sense, but I could tell he was really falling apart. It scared me to hear him like that. In our ten years of marriage, I had never heard him cry."

Marjorie nodded understandingly, encouraging Sara to continue. "I told him to get on the next plane," Sara explained. "No grant was so important that he should have to suffer like that. I know it was humiliating for him, but the next day he bought a ticket and came back to the States."

"So that's why he came back so suddenly," Marjorie broke in. "I always wondered. But you did spend the year in Argentina. What turned things around for Charles?"

Sara smiled. "Well, once Charles got back to familiar surroundings he regained his confidence. But he was never quite the same. Calling me and admitting his own neediness was the first time he had ever let me give to him. I think he was surprised that I didn't leave him or something, you know, for not being the perfectly strong, always in control man of the world." Sara's eyes filled with affectionate tears. "It just gave me the chance to love him more."

Several weeks after his disastrous first trip, Charles again booked a flight to Buenos Aires. This time, the entire family went together. Sara described the happy ending to the story. "We had arranged to stay in the home of an old college friend, an American who worked as a pediatrician in Buenos Aires. She agreed to let all four of us stay with her indefinitely and use her apartment as a home base until we could find a place of our own. She met us at the airport, welcomed us, took us to her apartment, fed us, drove us around. Within a few days, Charles had located an apartment. It was really amazing. When he made contact with the university's housing office, Charles swallowed his pride and carried out the negotiations in English, not Spanish!"

With the support of Sara and the children, Charles was able to figure out confusing signs, maps, forms, and customs. He had learned that he could not live his life wholly on his own, out of his own resources. None of us are that competent, that strong. We all need others. Charles had been fooled into thinking that by pretending to be perfect he was helping other people. He had fallen into the Messiah Trap, placing value on playing god in other people's lives. Facing the truth can be excruciatingly painful. But the phone call to Sara was the first time, since he sat as a frightened boy in a hospital lobby, that Charles had dared to rely on anyone else. He began to break free of the Messiah Trap and experience the two-sided reality of love.

During his year in Argentina, Charles learned over and over that he needed to open himself to other people. He realized that he could no longer live his life in isolation. He exchanged his false sense of strength for a tenacious bond of love. As he let others make a real difference to him, Charles let go of the vise grip he held around his own life. He learned to be vulnerable and to receive others into his own life.

This new ability to open himself to others and to let others into his life (the first side of love) did not make Charles into an overly dependent person. Instead, it freed Charles to give of himself in a new way (the second side of love).

Both sides of love, both the receptivity and the activity, involve risk. In the receptivity of love, we risk being vulnerable by opening ourselves to another person. We risk allowing that person to affect us, change us, and make our lives different than they would have been otherwise. The personal resources of those we love become a part of our own journeys. As we allow other people to break through our egocentric walls, we discard the idea that each of us is the only person in the world who matters. We risk finding ourselves in relationship to another person, rather than creating ourselves wholly through our own efforts. We risk giving up total control over our lives and pretending we are gods. This side of love, the receptive one, involves the risk of sharing our lives with others. We risk receiving or accepting the gift of other persons into our lives.

The second side of love, the active one, also involves risk. Here we risk offering ourselves and our personal resources to the other person. Sometimes our offerings are refused or misused. We risk allowing our lives to become a part of the other person's development and therefore out of our own control. We invest our time, energy, and talent not in our own egocentric interests but in the interests of another person, without any guarantee as to the outcome. We risk daring that our lives will be fulfilled as we live them for others. We risk offering ourselves as a gift for another.

We have used the word *gift* to describe both sides of love. It is risky to receive and to give gifts. When given a birthday present, we must accept it, receive it, open it, use it. To receive a gift is to open our lives to the insights and creativity of another person. When we give a gift, we risk offering the other person a small part of ourselves. We risk taking the effort to do for another person. We take the risk that we know them well enough to offer them something that can be of value in their life.

Love in Action

Marjorie glanced back into the living room at her brother-in-law. "Well, it is obvious that Charles has changed. This afternoon he asked me how I was doing and actually listened to my answer!"

Sara laughed. "You should see him at home. Not only has he supported me in going back to school, he actually volunteered to cook dinner on the nights I have class. Not that he's become a gourmet cook or anything, but it is the best food I have ever tasted. You know, I actually think he enjoys himself. We've heard him singing in the kitchen."

The sisters smiled in silence as they imagined the scene. Charles popped his head into the kitchen. "So what are you two whispering about?"

Sara stood up and wrapped her arms around him. "Oh, I was just telling Marjorie what a wonderful man you are."

Charles smiled and then turned to Marjorie. "There really have been a lot of changes for me this year. More than slides can capture. I used to think of the time I spent with the family as an interruption. Now it is my most valuable time."

Because Charles had experienced both sides of love, sharing his own life with those he loved was no longer a burden. Gone were the days he grudgingly volunteered for projects out of guilt or obligation. Now he really listened to others and let them make an impact on his life before he worked to give to them. There was no longer room for the arrogance and self-sufficiency that is fostered by the Messiah Trap. Instead of griping about how far behind he was in his work, Charles could go to bed satisfied that he had helped Sara type a paper or that he had been there at the kindergarten for his daughter's afternoon performance of "Peter Rabbit."

CHAPTER 7

Does God Love You Like an Attentive Parent?

But the steadfast love of God is from everlasting to everlasting.
—Psalm 103:17

God is love, and whoever abides in love abides in God, and God abides in them.
—1 John 4:16

Does God love us? And if God loves us, does that make any difference to our lives down in trenches, when we face loss and heartache? We believe that God's love is more than a pious sentiment, a small fire by which to warm ourselves into a deluded sense of security. It is God's love that offers us a practical, down-to-earth alternative to the destructive, yet seductive, lies of the Messiah Trap.

Look at the Birds of the Air

Cheryl had lived in a fog ever since Heidi died. It took all her strength to keep one foot moving in front of the other. Not even her work offered Cheryl an escape from the world of feelings as it had in the past. Late one afternoon, following a committee meeting, Cheryl found herself driving toward the parking lot above a section of beach that Heidi had loved.

Heidi had found this special place and visited it often before the cancer forced her to bed. This small, sandy stretch of beach below rocky Pacific cliffs became a natural sanctuary where Heidi would walk and sing a hymn or pray. Cheryl vividly remembered the youth group's cookout at Heidi's beach the previous summer. Heidi had been so excited to share her special place with her friends.

The car seemed to drive itself toward that sacred spot. In a daze, Cheryl parked her car and began walking down the long wooden steps to the beach. About halfway down, Cheryl left the walkway and crawled out on a huge boulder where she could watch the tide slowly go out. Her mind was blank, dull with pain. Cheryl thought to herself, "I'm glad that, for a few minutes, I'm not pretending to feel in control of all of this." Her mind reviewed her various tasks: leading worship, teaching, moderating committee meetings. Cheryl sat numb, grateful not to be working, not to be in one of her many roles of responsibility.

Then something darted across the sand, catching Cheryl's attention. It was a bird. Cheryl noticed several more. She watched as the gulls and the sandpipers worked their way down the beach after the receding tide. The birds would take a few steps, then stoop to poke their bills into the sand. Up they would come with a worm or small crustacean. Quite a find for dinner! It seemed like an easy, effortless life. Walk on a beach, find food, eat, walk, find more food. No responsibility, no self-doubt, no guilt.

Jesus' words in Matthew 6:25–30 began to whisper in Cheryl's mind along with the lapping of the waves. She had read those words many times and had even preached one of her first sermons on the passage:

> Therefore I tell you, do not be anxious about your life, what you shall eat or what you shall drink, nor about your body, what you shall put on. Is not life more than food, and the body more than clothing? Look at the birds of the air. They neither sow nor reap nor gather into barns, and yet God feeds them. Are you not of more value than they? And which of you by being anxious can

add one cubit to your span of life? And why are you anxious about clothing? Consider the lilies of the field, how they grow; they neither toil nor spin; yet I tell you, even Solomon in all his glory was not arrayed like one of these. But if God so clothes the grass of the field, which is alive today and tomorrow is thrown into the oven, will God not much more clothe you, O people of little faith?

Cheryl was amazed as she suddenly saw the beach, the sand, the water, the sky, the birds all as part of one gift, God's gift of life. The wind blows, the sea comes in and goes out, the birds fly and look for food. All this life is a gift from God. No work, no burnout, just living from the resources provided by God. The gulls and the sandpipers seem to avoid feeling obligated to control the world or to take on more responsibility than was theirs.

"Why can't I take life one moment at a time, like these birds?" Cheryl asked herself. "Why do I worry and fret about everything? How I wish I *could* believe that God cares for me like the birds and the flowers!"

We believe Christians can be freed from the Messiah Trap only through a change in their image of God. The release and empowerment so desperately needed by the person caught in the Messiah Trap are made possible when that person genuinely believes that God is love and lives in the power of God's love. Of course, talk about God as love is familiar to Christians. It can be found throughout Scripture as well as in Christian liturgies, hymns, and devotional literature. For several reasons, however, we often do not take this talk about God as love seriously and do not recognize its consequences.

First, we don't always trust the power of love in our own lives. We all tend to create security for ourselves through our own actions. Let's face it, in many ways love is a much riskier way of being, acting, and relating than is the exertion of coercive power or the sacrifice of ourselves to someone else who controls us. In love one has let go of the need to control the significance of one's life. In love, one offers oneself to another and finds one's true identity in vulnerability and mutuality, not in self-control and self-sufficiency or self-abandonment and self-destruction. Sometimes it is difficult for us to take the risk of love. We need to begin to trust in the power of love. We must dare to believe that love is the greatest power in the universe, for God *is* love.

Second, Christians have often viewed God, not in terms of love, but in terms of the idolatrous images of God discussed earlier. Unconsciously, many of us have grown up with a picture of God as supreme, coercive power, a power that does anything to anyone at any time. But that picture of God is not really drawn from Scripture, certainly not from the ultimate example of God's power: the life, death, and resurrection of Jesus Christ. Instead, images of God as Absent Parent or Abusive Parent come from our own worst use of power, our own inappropriate ways of treating one another. Isn't it high time that we discovered a new image of God, one based on the truth that God *is* love?

Finally, we have been hindered by our tendency to think of God's love as one of God's attributes or characteristics among others. Many of us have grown up talking about God's wisdom, God's eternity, God's power, God's love, and so on, in the same way that we talk about a person's attributes or characteristics: their height, weight, hair color, eye color, and so on. If we begin by thinking of God's love as a separate quality from God's power, eternity, and wisdom, it will be very difficult to reconcile God's presence with the evil in the world.

A New Image of God

Cheryl, wanting to be closer to the sand and water, climbed down to the beach and took her shoes off. The sand wrapped around her tired feet. She walked slowly along the deserted beach. She was headed nowhere in particular but was willing to begin a new journey. The sun had become a huge flaming ball in the west, bathing the sand, the water, and the cliffs with a warm, soft glow.

Once again Cheryl thought of Heidi. She remembered how limber and quick Heidi had been playing volleyball on this same beach; how reluctant she had been to get into the cold water; how grateful she was for the warmth of the bonfire. Heidi had told Cheryl that God had given her special strength on this beach, strength she needed to face her illness and impending death. Cheryl wondered if such strength could ever be hers. Maybe she could also find help on this narrow stretch of sand. Hot tears ran unchecked down Cheryl's face, the first truly heartfelt tears she had shed for Heidi since her death.

The problem of evil was not a theoretical puzzle or a philosophical brainteaser for Cheryl. It was flesh and blood and tears. She cried out to God, "I don't understand why all this happened! Why did Heidi have to die? Why am I so overwhelmed? Where are you, anyway? Don't you care about all of this?"

As do many who view God as an Absent Parent, Cheryl interpreted tragic loss as evidence that God is not active in the world. Cheryl was looking for a "power" answer, where God intervenes and does something coercively about evil. Her eyes were searching for signs of a "power" God and were thereby blinded to God's "love" answer. As we see in Jesus Christ, God's action in the world is not coercion but redeeming love.

Christians caught in the Messiah Trap, like Cheryl, need to discover an image of God as *pure, unbounded love,* to use the phrase from Charles Wesley's hymn "Love Divine, All Loves Excelling." Love is not one of God's characteristics but is the very nature of God. Love that is absolutely pure and utterly boundless is the one attribute or characteristic that makes God God. God's power is not something separate from God's love, it is the power of God's pure, unbounded love. God's eternity is not a separate characteristic alongside love. Instead, God's eternity is the everlastingness of God's pure, unbounded love. God's wisdom is nothing but the vision of new possibilities available in God's pure, unbounded love. God *is* love.

A way to begin to develop this new image of God would be to apply the definition of love suggested in the previous chapter to

God. God's very nature is expressed in what we have called the receptive and active sides of love. To say God *is* love means that God allows all people (as well as all of God's creatures) to make a real difference in God's life, and, because of the real difference they make, God acts toward all people so as to assist them to develop fully as persons. Once again, it may help to personalize this definition, for God does not love an anonymous crowd called "all people." God loves each of us as the unique persons we are. So, to say God *is* love means that God allows Carmen and Mark and Jenny and Cheryl and Charles and Maria and Ronda to make a real difference in God's life, and, because of the real difference each one of them makes, God acts toward Carmen and Mark and Jenny and Cheryl and Charles and Maria and Ronda so as to assist each one to develop fully as a person. (The two sides of God's love will be explored in this chapter and in the following one.)

Since God is love, God wills nothing but the full development of each of us. Like an Attentive Parent, God acts in love by giving us the space and resources to create ourselves freely. Evil and suffering are not results of God's activity but are the tragic consequences of the limits and misuse of the world God has given us. For God to intervene and simply wipe away evil and suffering would be coercion, not love. We need to stop evading the reality of evil and suffering by trying to blame them on God.

Where do evil and suffering come from? They are the consequences of a finite world, populated by creatures with free will, who have marred the world through their sin. Sometimes we create evil and suffering through the misuse of our freedom. In other cases, such as Heidi's death, we suffer the limitations of our finite world. But in no circumstance is God the creator of evil and suffering, for God is pure, unbounded love.

The Receptivity of God's Love

As Cheryl walked and wept, she began to imagine that she was watching Heidi on the deserted beach. In her imagination, Cheryl watched Heidi skip and dance by the water's edge at sunset with the gulls and sandpipers. Cheryl realized that Heidi was also part of the one great gift of life. She was as much a part of God's gift of life as was the sand and the water and the air and the birds.

Cheryl continued to weep as she thought, "Heidi, dear as you were to me, you were not my possession. You were God's gift." Cheryl realized that she had wanted to control Heidi's life and was frustrated when she didn't have the power to make things happen as she wanted. Even though Cheryl had wanted something good for Heidi, Cheryl had still wanted control. When she couldn't have control, Cheryl had become enraged. "That rage was transferred to God," Cheryl admitted to herself. "I wanted God to do what I couldn't, and when God didn't, I doubted God's presence."

It was God's love that fed the gulls and sandpipers, that moved the air and brought the tide in and out each day. It wasn't Cheryl's ability or effort. And it was God's love that met Heidi on her walks along the beach, preparing her for her departure from this world. In Cheryl's imagination, she saw Heidi's figure surrounded by the golden light of the setting sun. Heidi was made golden by the light. Although Heidi was dead to Cheryl, she was still surrounded by the inextinguishable light of God's love. For the first time, Cheryl saw that Heidi was not really gone but was held in God's hands forever.

God is not an Absent Parent. God is not indifferent to us. We each make a real difference to God. This means that God allows our lives, our interests, feelings, likes, dislikes, plans, and wishes to become a part of God's life, a part of God's interests, feelings, and plans.

When we love another person, we don't literally become that other person, we remain the unique individuals that we are. However, when we love another person, we do make them a part of our lives. We allow their experience to become a part of our experience. Our field of concern is extended to encompass their lives. In the same way, to say God allows our lives to become a part of God's life does not mean that we are God or become God. We are not God and we don't become God. But God does allow our experience to become a part of God's experience. God's field of concern is extended to encompass our lives.

When we rejoice over the birth of a child or a well-deserved promotion or the unrewarded kindness another person shows us, God also rejoices, for God makes our rejoicing a part of God's experience. When we grieve over the tragic deaths of innocent people, God also grieves, for the loss of those persons is also shared by God. To say God *is* love is to dare to believe that, far from being the most impassive, aloof, and unaffected person, God is the most receptive, feeling, and involved person. God is not untouched by the lives of others. Instead, God is most open to others.

If God's love is receptive, just as our human love is, then what is the difference between God and us? The difference is that God's love is pure and unbounded, while our love is not. It is not that others make a difference and are included within our human lives and are not in God's life. The difference is that God loves *all* other persons. God allows absolutely every person to make a difference to God. God includes within God's life the lives, feelings, and experiences of all persons. Each of us loves on a much more limited, partial basis. We allow the lives of only a tiny handful of persons to make a real difference to us. Even the most loving among us includes within our lives the interests of only a few people closest to us: family members, spouses, friends, co-workers. God's love is infinitely greater than our love because it is utterly boundless. It excludes or overlooks no person. It is absolutely pure. Our human love always tends to be mixed with selfish motives or self-negating behavior. We never truly love other people with complete purity. God does, and that is what makes God different from us.

To say that God's love, like ours, has a receptive side means that we have an effect on God. Does this mean that we change God? No and yes. Nothing we are or do can change the fact that God is God. Nothing we are or do can change the fact that God is love. Nothing we are or do can change the fact that God's love is all-powerful, eternal, and all-wise. In other words, God's character, God's personality, God's "Godness" are utterly unchangeable and are not affected by us.

What is changed, although this is not quite the right word since we usually think of change being a weakness, is God's actual experience. It is not so much change as it is involvement. God is aware of us as we are. The alternative would be to say that God would remain literally the same whether we were rejoicing or grieving, honest or dishonest, burned-out or healthy. That is the idolatrous image of God as Absent Parent again. While God would be aware of us no matter what, how God is actually involved in our lives is different, depending on whether we are rejoicing or grieving, honest or dishonest, burned-out or healthy. God's love addresses us as we really are.

"God is not absent, the way my father was," Cheryl thought as she basked in the golden light of the setting sun. "My cries do not fall on deaf ears. No. God loves me. God suffers the evil of the world along with me. The evil we do to each other and the tragic suffering that comes our way are evil and tragic to God as well. Heidi's suffering was suffering felt by God. My pain is God's pain. The burnout and guilt that have hindered my growth have been a frustration of what God wants for me."

Like Cheryl, we need to look in a different direction when we think about evil and suffering. As Cheryl began to see through the eyes of love, she no longer looked at evil and suffering and asked if God was the cause. She no longer asked why God didn't do something to prevent Heidi from dying in the first place. Instead, she was able to see God as her Attentive Parent as she prayed, "God, how do you want to redeem this tragic situation? What new creation might come about out of Heidi's illness and death?" Her attention had been shifted from a backward-looking question about God's actions in the past to a forward-looking question about what she and God might do in the future. Her question was no longer "Why did this happen?" but "What can now happen?" This can be our question too.

A Biblical Portrait of God's Love

Only the image of God as pure, unbounded love does justice to the God found in Scripture. In 1 John we find what is probably the simplest, yet most profound, sentence in the Bible: "God is love" (1 John 4:16). The sentence does not read, "Sometimes God acts toward us lovingly, other times with indifference or hatred." It says God *is* love, always. The sentence does not read, "Part of God's character is love, but God is also power and eternity and wisdom." It says God *is* love, period.

Of course, as many of us discovered even as children in Sunday school, some passages in the Bible seem to depict God as violent and vindictive. Many of these passages are found in Old Testament stories, but some occur in the New Testament as well. How we are to deal with these warlike images of God raises a number of difficult questions about the nature of Scripture, human history, human perceptions of God, God's revelation, and so on. While we can't deal fully with these issues in this book, we do want to say two things. (1) It is our conviction that as Christians we are to read all of Scripture from the perspective of God's self-revelation in Jesus Christ. Scripture must be allowed to interpret Scripture, and it is the love of God embodied in the life, death, and resurrection of Jesus of Nazareth that clarifies and completes everything the prophets and apostles say. (2) While the love of God was perfectly revealed in Jesus Christ, the Old Testament also proclaims God's love and prepares us for the story of Jesus. For this reason, it might be helpful to look at a portrait of God's love painted in the Old Testament.

Psalm 103 is a hymn of praise for God's love. It begins, as do many other psalms, with a call to the people of God to praise: "Bless the Lord, O my soul; and all that is within me bless God's holy name" (Psalm 103:1). Verse 2 invites us to praise God for "all God's benefits." Then follows a list of what God does for the people: "forgives all your iniquity" and "heals all your diseases" (3); "redeems your life from the Pit" and "crowns you with steadfast love and mercy" (4); "satisfies you with good as long as you live, so that your youth is renewed like the eagle's" (5).

After a brief reminder of God's acts of love for the people of Israel in verses 6 and 7, the body of the psalm focuses on two of God's benefits from the list: forgiveness and redemption. Forgiveness and redemption are the two chief accomplishments of God's pure, unbounded love in our lives. Forgiveness has to do with how God responds to our sin. Redemption has to do with how God responds to our mortality. We choose to sin; we do not choose to die, that is our nature. We are responsible for our sin; we are not responsible for our mortality. In each case, God responds to us in an unexpected way. The psalmist contrasts how we, humanly speaking, might expect God to treat us and how God, in truth, relates to us in love.

Psalm 103:8–13 deals with sin and forgiveness. Sin is a refusal to be the persons God created us to be. Sin is a turning away from God, from our truest selves, and from other people around us. Because of our turning away, we might expect God to refuse to have anything more to do with us. Because we have rejected God's gift to us, it would make (human) sense for God to reject us. But God does the unexpected. "God does not deal with us according to our sins, nor requite us according to our iniquities" (10). Instead, as parents pity their children, so God pities, has mercy, on us. Far from rejecting us because we are sinners, God forgives us. God refuses to allow our rejection of God's gift of life to separate us from God. God continues to accept and love us even in the midst of our sin. "For as the heavens are high above the earth, so great is God's steadfast love toward those who fear God; as far as the east is from the west, so far does God remove our transgressions from us" (11–12). God accepts us in spite of our sin. We are called to accept God's acceptance of us, to accept the gift of God's forgiving love.

Mortality and redemption are the focus in verses 14 through 18. The psalmist speaks about our human frailty, our mortality. "For God knows our frame; God remembers that we are dust. Our days are like grass; we flourish like a flower of the field; the wind passes over it, and it is gone, and its place knows it no more" (14–16). The point is not just that we die. More important is the fact that everything we do threatens to become meaningless, as transient and frail as dry grass. Our lives would seem to have no lasting value or significance.

One could think of mortality or transience as a question of memory. A person continues to have some meaning, even after they are dead, and their lives continue to have some influence, if other people remember them. When we remember something, even though it is past, it is still included within our lives, it still has a presence with us and a reality for us.

Now let's try an experiment with memory, to better understand Psalm 103. There are some five billion people alive on this planet at this moment. How many of their names would every one of us recognize? Probably a dozen or so, some world leaders and celebrities. Most people alive in the world right now are not known to us and have no part in our lives.

What if we asked the same question about people who lived a hundred years ago? How many names of people who lived in 1890 would every one of us recognize? Maybe a few: a president of the United States, or perhaps a famous author or musician or scientist. What if we asked how many people who lived a thousand or two thousand years ago we had all heard of? Maybe only one or two: Jesus of Nazareth or maybe Julius Caesar.

The point is that if we expect to gain a kind of immortality by becoming famous and being remembered by many people after we are dead, we are in for disappointment. Each of us will be remembered by a few people for some years after we die. Our lives will have made an impact on them. But sooner or later, those people will also die, and eventually we will be forgotten by all human beings. Once we are totally forgotten, what is the value of our lives? Where has the significance of our actions and words gone? Has it simply ceased to be? This is the problem of mortality.

Psalm 103 has an answer to the problem of mortality. "But the steadfast love of God is from everlasting to everlasting upon those who fear God, and God's righteousness to children's children, to those who keep the covenant and remember to do God's commandments" (17–18). While all human beings may forget us, God will never forget us. Just as God refuses to allow our sin to separate us from God, so God refuses to let us slip away into oblivion because of our mortality. It is God's love, not our deeds or words or fame, that lasts forever. We are forever held in the tender arms of God's love. The significance of our lives can never pass away, because

God makes our lives a part of the everlasting, loving life of God. God accepts us and this acceptance is redemption. God's love "redeems us from the Pit" (4). All we need do is accept the redemptive action of God's love.

Psalm 103 is a powerful testimony to the love of God, a love that refuses to let go of us but instead forgives our sins and redeems our transient lives. Despite our sinful rejection of God, of our truest selves, and of others, we are accepted, forgiven, offered a gift of new life and wholeness. Despite our mortality, God redeems us forever, offering an eternal life and everlasting meaning in the love of God, from which we can never be separated.

God, Our Attentive Parent

Digging her toes deeply into the wet sand, Cheryl recalled Heidi's cheerfulness and courage in new situations, her generous attitude toward others, the way she helped Jimmy, the slow boy in the group, without looking down on him, her love of music and the songs she would sing at the nursing home. Cheryl realized that all those gifts Heidi had offered so freely were not lost at all. Heidi's kindness lived on in Jimmy. Heidi's music lived on in Mrs. Shields at the nursing home. Cheryl thought of the many conversations she had had with Heidi's friends and family since the funeral and how the impact of Heidi's life still continued in the people she had touched.

Heidi was dead and Cheryl's tears flowed as a tribute to how much she would miss her. But Cheryl's shock and despair over Heidi's death were softened and melted by the golden glow of the setting sun, gently swept from her by the breeze, and carried out to sea on the ebbing tide. Cheryl thought to herself, "I have been afraid to let go of Heidi, as if she would slip away from me. But now I see that I must let go of my fantasy of control. Heidi is not my possession and she is not mine to keep." Tears again welled up in her eyes as, with gratitude, she realized, "Because God loves us both, I will never truly lose Heidi. She was a gift from God offered to the world for sixteen short years but treasured by God for eternity."

When our expectations have changed, then we are able to see what was there all the time. We see God as our Attentive Parent. As pure, unbounded love, God acts all-powerfully in the world to redeem evil and suffering. God not only suffers with us. In each moment of suffering, brokenness, and evil, God's love offers us the possibility of re-creation through forgiveness. In each moment, God's love gives us a new chance to become ourselves. The final truth about life is that we are unconditionally, eternally accepted by God, not because of what we have done but simply because God is love.

Nothing we do or fail to do can change the fact that God loves us. Our pain, our success, our suffering, our joy, our whole lives, everything we do and are become part of God's everlasting life. The promise of God's love is that we are valuable and that nothing valuable is ever lost in God. We are released. We can let go knowing that God, our Attentive Parent, holds us in love.

In her imagination, Cheryl watched Heidi, now far down the beach, turn and wave good-bye. Cheryl raised her hand and waved in return. As the vision passed, Cheryl found herself waving up at the empty cliffs. She was startled by the water on her feet, as if she had never felt such coolness before. The warm, gentle breeze played in her hair, and her whole body was surrounded by the pink glow of the now set sun. "I have been numb for a long time," Cheryl smiled to herself, gratefully enjoying her return to a world of feeling. "I am a part of all this." Again her eyes filled with tears, this time tears of gratitude, not sorrow. She thought of all God's gifts at that very moment: air to breathe, light with which to see, color, the incessant sound of the sea, her mind, her memories. Cheryl saw herself as a part of God's great gift of life. Just as the water and the breeze and the gulls and sandpipers and Heidi were God's gifts of love, so, too, was Cheryl.

To see that God loves us as our Attentive Parent offers *release* to the person caught in the first lie of the Messiah Trap ("If I don't do it, it won't get done"). No longer do we feel compelled to do something about evil because we don't see God involved. As we develop spiritual eyes able to recognize God's powerful work of love, we can be freed from the image of God as Absent Parent and replace it with an image of God as Attentive Parent, the pure and boundless lover of all. Along with Cheryl, we can recover a childlike sense that life is a gift, not a burden or an assignment.

God's love offers us the possibility of being released from our addictive styles of working and helping. If God loves us in a way that redeems and re-creates the world, then our working and helping are but a small part of a much larger whole. If all our work is made part of God's everlasting life, then our small efforts for others really are of eternal value, however fragile they look in human eyes. If we succeed in helping someone, then that act of re-creation is never lost, for it is made a part of God's own act of re-creation.

Cheryl saw that her actions, her work in the church, even the many hours no one on the board knew about were surrounded and contained in God's love, just like Heidi's kindness and music. Cheryl realized that she was not the center of the world. The ebb and flow of the tides were not her responsibility. It was not Cheryl's task to feed gulls and sandpipers or to make the breeze blow or the sun set. All that was the activity of God's love.

We are not God and we need not be God. We do not need to put ourselves in the place of God the Absent Parent, for that place has been filled all along with God our Attentive Parent. The final meaning of our helping activities lies not in us but in God's love. Those we seek to help also become part of God's life. In God, their lives find lasting wholeness and meaning. None of us is solely responsible for the world. God has the final responsibility. And the receptivity and activity of God's love is never visible in the obvious way in which coercive power is visible. As illustrated in Jesus Christ, God's love bears and redeems all. Because God's love never lets go of anything or anyone, we are offered the grace of letting go, of releasing the burden of the world.

Like Cheryl, those of us caught in the first lie of the Messiah Trap try to be in control of the world and insist that we are responsible for eliminating the evil in the world. To trust that God loves us is to give up this unrealistic responsibility and to relax in our rightful place in creation.

Cheryl's face reflected the lingering glow of the sun. "For the first time since Heidi's death, I don't feel alone. God is here." As she escaped the Messiah Trap, Cheryl was able to recognize that God was as near to her as the pink light that caressed her. She prayed, "God, I release control over my work. I accept your love." She felt the burden of bitterness, anger, and a false sense of responsibility recede with the tide. Release was hers. She was as free as a bird, as free as the gulls and the sandpipers feeding without anxiety or worry in the sand near her. Raising her arms to the sky, Cheryl welcomed the love of God.

CHAPTER 8

Does God Love You Like a Nurturing Parent?

For God so loved the world that God gave the only Son, that whoever believes in him should not perish but have eternal life. For God sent the Son into the world, not to condemn the world, but that the world might be saved through him.
—John 3:16–17

While the person caught in the first lie of the Messiah Trap suffers from the distortion that God is absent, the person caught in the second lie incorrectly views God as abusive. This second lie declares, "Everyone else's needs take priority over mine," so that we begin to believe that God considers our needs to be of little, if any, importance. God appears unpredictable, cruel, and demanding. Not only are we to sacrifice all that we have, our rightful service to God involves the destruction of who we are.

Ronda had fallen prey to this lie. She no longer believed that God valued her as a person. Although she was unsure about what she had done wrong, she secretly feared that it had been something terrible and the abuse she endured was deserved. Questioning God or expressing any anger about her situation filled her with terror. "What if God punishes me even more for these sinful thoughts," she cried to herself at night. "I must not be angry at God. My problem is that I am too rebellious."

In the counseling sessions with her husband, Sid, Ronda tried to hide her anger and fear. She was terrified that she would expose herself as a terrible sinner, undeserving of God's forgiveness. The marriage counselor began one of the sessions by giving both Sid and Ronda a series of homework assignments. "The point of these assignments," the counselor said, "is to help you both be more honest about your feelings and needs." Ronda nodded in compliance as her stomach twisted into a knot. She didn't think anyone, not Sid or the counselor and certainly not God, could handle her being truly honest about how she felt. "How I feel is unworthy," she agonized inside. But to the counselor she smiled, "Oh, certainly. I think these exercises could be helpful."

The next week seemed busier than ever, certainly much too busy to deal with the assignment. But the afternoon before the next session, Ronda sat down to address the task, not because she wanted to, but because she couldn't face disappointing the counselor.

The first assignment was to write a list of ten things Ronda liked about herself. Ronda sat for thirty minutes. She began four or five lists but crumpled them all up and threw them on the floor. Rage at Sid and God would sweep over her, followed by guilt and shame. "I'm such an awful person," she scowled at the blank page. "How can I come up with any good qualities?"

A Biblical Portrait of God's Love

The theme of one of Jesus' most familiar parables is that God accepts us even when we feel unacceptable. This story, recorded in Luke 15:11–32, is usually called the parable of the prodigal son. A prodigal is someone who gives away what they have freely and without restraint. If this is true, then there is good reason to rename the story the parable of the prodigal father. Although the younger son certainly does squander his inheritance, it is really the father who gives freely and unconditionally, who transcends all the normal rules in his attitude toward his son.

The story is well known. A young man asks his father for his rightful inheritance, which the father gives him, and sets off to make his way in the world.

> There was a man who had two sons; and the younger of them said to his father, "Father, give me the share of property that falls to me." And the father divided his living between them. Not many days later, the younger son gathered all he had and took his journey into a far country (Luke 15:11–13).

In Jesus' day, the purpose of such an inheritance was to allow the son to set himself up with a house and land, thereby providing the basis for his future livelihood. This son, of course, is reckless and wastes it all.

> [T]here he squandered his property in loose living. And when he had spent everything, a great famine arose in that country, and he began to be in want. So he went and joined himself to one of the citizens of that country, who sent him into his fields to feed swine. And he would have gladly fed on the pods that the swine ate; and no one gave him anything (13–16).

The younger son had sunk as low as possible for a Jew in Jesus' time. Instead of using his inheritance to build himself a life, he has lost all and is reduced to feeding pigs, in violation of the laws of purity of his faith. He comes to his senses and realizes that while he starves, even the lowliest servant of his father has plenty to eat. The younger son decides to return to his father and confess the error of his ways. He is willing to forfeit his former role as son and take on the role of a servant.

> But when he came to himself he said, "How many of my father's hired servants have bread enough and to spare, but I perish here with hunger! I will arise and go to my father, and I will say to him, 'Father, I have sinned

against heaven and before you; I am no longer worthy to
be called your son; treat me as one of your hired servants.' " And he arose and came to his father (17–20).

According to the laws of the day, the father had already done
everything required of him. In giving his younger son his inheritance, the father had fulfilled his duty to the boy. The father was
under no legal obligation to receive his son back again. But the father in the parable does not act in accordance with human stan-
dards of justice and fairness. The father goes and does something
shocking, something prodigal. He acts as if nothing had happened.
He doesn't reject the young man but instead accepts him back.

Before the son could deliver his carefully rehearsed confession
and apology, the father had accepted him back. "But while the
younger son was yet at a distance, his father saw him and had com-
passion, and ran and embraced him and kissed him" (20). The son
was completely unacceptable, legally, yet before any apology the
father loved him. The father's love was not conditional upon the
son shaping up, reforming and promising never to do anything
like that again. The father's love was unconditional. His love was
not a response to the son's confession and apology; it preceded it.

Even this doesn't exhaust the father's generosity. Instead of
graciously accepting the son's offer to become a hired servant, the
father welcomes the young man back as a son in the fullest sense.

But the father said to his servants, "Bring quickly the
best robe, and put it on him; and put a ring on his hand,
and shoes on his feet; and bring the fatted calf and kill it,
and let us eat and be merry; for this my son was dead,
and is alive again; he was lost and is found." And they
began to make merry (22–24).

The father rewards irresponsibility with a huge banquet; reckless, destructive selfishness with love and support.

According to the expectations of Jesus' audience, it is only the
elder brother who has any sense. He alone complains that the father's prodigality toward the younger son is inappropriate.

Now his elder son was in the field; and as he came and drew near to the house, he heard music and dancing. And he called one of the servants and asked what this meant. And he said to him, "Your brother has come, and your father has killed the fatted calf, because he has received him safe and sound." But the elder son was angry and refused to go in. His father came out and entreated him, but he answered his father, "Lo, these many years I have served you, and I have never disobeyed your command; yet you never gave me a kid, that I might make merry with my friends. But when this son of yours came, who has devoured your living with prostitutes, you killed for him the fatted calf!" (25–30)

Of course, Jesus' point in telling the story is to undercut our ordinary assumptions about God's love. The father is the God figure in the parable. Jesus is saying that God acts toward us as the father in the parable did toward his younger son. Even before we have confessed and apologized to God for our rejection of God's gift of life to us, even before we have been able to reform ourselves, God is already seeking us and loving us, ever ready to restore our lives. God does not act in accordance with our human sense of fairness. God does not count the cost first but loves us enough to give all for us.

And the father said to his elder son, "You are always with me, and all that is mine is yours. It was fitting to make merry and be glad, for this your brother was dead, and is alive; he was lost, and is found" (31–32).

We have all probably heard sermons warning us against being like the younger son. Indeed, we should not be wasteful with God's many gifts to us. Perhaps a more difficult message of Jesus' parable is that *we should treat ourselves and other people as the father treated the younger son.* Perhaps we are in greater danger of being like the elder rather than the younger brother. The Christian caught in the Messiah Trap treats herself or himself the way the older son wished his father had treated the younger son: rejecting and punishing him as unworthy.

This parable, like Psalm 103, proclaims the utter purity and boundlessness of God's love. Like the younger son, we make a real difference to God. We can never travel so far that we are not still surrounded by God's care and love. No matter how much we have fallen short of our truest selves, God our Nurturing Parent still loves us, seeks us, and accepts us as daughters and sons. God is ever ready to act toward us to fill our lives with the joyous and plentiful feast of love, freedom, and wholeness.

"My Name Is Written on His Hands"

Unable to make any progress on her assignment, Ronda got up from the kitchen table. She paced around the living room for a few minutes looking out at the light rain. Then she went over to the stereo. Ronda hoped music might distract her from her frustration and anger for a while. As she was rummaging through her drawer of cassette tapes, she came across one she had not played in months. It was a collection of hymns recorded by a British orchestra and choral society. She put it in the tape deck.

Ronda's best memories of her religious upbringing were connected with the hymns she had learned as a child. She could sing from memory a good fifty or so hymns. As an adult, she found a wealth of encouragement in hymns. Something about the great hymns of the church spoke more powerfully to Ronda than did sermons or even Bible stories.

Ronda turned on the tape player and allowed the familiar sounds to fill her living room. But this Tuesday afternoon, Ronda was not listening very closely. The hymns offered nothing more than background noise. Flopping on the couch, she allowed her mind to wander.

But then Ronda's attention was caught by the hymn "Arise, My Soul, Arise," the tune to which had always been one of her favorites. As she began to listen to the words, she was moved by the end of the first verse. The hymn made such an impression that Ronda went to the piano bench and searched through several beginning piano and trumpet books until she found the battered old hymnal her home church had given to her when she went off to college. Ronda sat down at the piano and slowly picked out the chords of the hymn and sang the words softly.

Arise, my soul, arise;
Shake off thy guilty fears.
The bleeding sacrifice
In my behalf appears.
Before the throne my surety stands,
Before the throne my surety stands,
My name is written on his hands.

Ronda remembered having been put off by the bloody metaphors in this hymn as a teenager. It was not that she doubted the reality or the importance of Jesus' suffering and death. But it made her uncomfortable to think and sing about it. This Tuesday afternoon, it was not the talk of blood that impressed Ronda. Instead, the message of empowerment in the hymn came to Ronda like water to a thirsty person in a desert.

As Ronda pictured in her mind Jesus' form on the cross, she could see her name inscribed on Jesus' hands. There, indelibly written into the flesh of God incarnate were the letters R-O-N-D-A. Ronda's mind was overwhelmed with the realization that the universe was different, God was different, because she, Ronda, had been born and lived on this earth. Because her name and her life had been imprinted onto God's incarnate life, nothing in the universe could ever change the fact that she had lived. Nothing and no one could deny her value as a person. If she mattered to no one else in the world, Ronda mattered to God, for her name was written on the hands of God.

The Activity of God's Love

In the definition of human love proposed earlier, the receptive side of love sets the foundation for the active side of love. The same is true for God's pure, unbounded love. Because of the real difference each person makes to God, because God is different for the inclusion of each person's experience into God's experience, God acts toward all persons so as to assist them in becoming full persons. God's love is not only supremely receptive, it is also supremely active.

When we truly love another person, our actions toward them are not coercive. Likewise, the active side of God's love does not coerce us. When we say that God acts to assist us to become fully ourselves, this does not mean that God lives our lives for us or that God waves a magic wand over us. Such action, however well intentioned, would be an imposition and would not respect our freedom. One can "coerce" a table into being. One can take lumber and (within limits) simply turn the lumber into a table. But one cannot do that with human beings. If people are to become, to change, to grow, they must freely make the decisions that lead to growth. This is true of our relationships to our friends, our spouses, our children. It is also true of God's relationship to us.

The active side of God's love is the opposite of the idolatrous image of God as Abusive Parent. The abuser acts toward others, not for the other person's own best interests, but for the sake of the abuser, to give him or her a sense of power and significance. God does not act in this way. The active side of God's love is completely self-giving, other affirming. God does not act to make God better, God is only concerned that each of us becomes ourselves, to the extent that is possible in a world where our freedom is limited by that of other persons. God's actions are designed to open up possibilities for us, not to close them down. God's actions represent greater freedom for us, not more bondage. God's actions are designed to make us whole.

Sitting at the piano, Ronda saw beyond her image of God as an abuser. God really did love her, enough to allow her life to touch God's, to become a part of God's. God's hands are not fists, Ronda realized, but hands that bear the scars of love and bear them gladly. She saw that her view of God as a vindictive punisher of the least of her misdeeds had been an idol. With tears of joy running down her face, Ronda sang the closing words of "Arise, My Soul, Arise":

With confidence I now draw nigh,
With confidence I now draw nigh,
And, "Father, Abba, Father," cry.

She could address God in the most intimate, parental terms of trust. As her Nurturing Parent, God was not to be feared. Nor did she have to prove her goodness to God. God already loved Ronda so much. She felt that God had reached out to her in love through the hymn, holding her like a nurturing parent. All Ronda had to do was to accept that love and let it work healing in her life.

If God does not coerce us into becoming richer and fuller persons, what does the active side of God's love amount to? Consider an analogy. Tender young tomato plants need rich soil, lots of sunlight, water, and eventually support, a stake, for example. What do tender, growing persons need? As we become ourselves, as we grow more whole and healthy, we need three things. First, we need unconditional acceptance. We need some other person to affirm our value unconditionally. We need someone to accept us in a way that is not dependent on our actions, whether for good or ill. Second, we need to catch a vision of the persons we might become. We need to find an image of ourselves as whole, healthy people. Third, we need to be given space and support as we strive and grow toward this new image of ourselves. We need others to give us the room and freedom to grow, not to try to dominate our lives or coerce us into growth. But we also need these other persons to share their lives with us, offer their personal resources for our use as we grow. We can't grow without space. Neither can we grow to healthy selves without supportive relationships to others.

God's pure, unbounded love offers us all three. In the receptive side of God's love we find unconditional acceptance. No matter what we have been or done, no matter how cruel others have been to us or how cruel we have been to ourselves, no matter how unimportant other people seem to think we are, we are of infinite value to God, because God makes our lives a part of God's very own life.

The active side of God's love provides the other two necessities for growth. God offers each of us a vision of wholeness, a new image of self toward which we can strive. God sets this vision of wholeness before us in Scripture (above all in the wholeness of human life represented by Jesus Christ), in the worshiping life of the church, and in the depths of our minds, hearts, and personal experience. God's love is active in all these ways. In each, we feel the gentle drawing power of our own redeemed and whole selves.

God's love also gives us the space and the support we need to act on this new vision of ourselves. God does not coerce us. God does not do things to us through the exertion of power. God's love opens up space and freedom for us. God's love makes room for our growth. But God's love also supports us as we grow. Because we know that God loves us and accepts us into God's life no matter what, we are encouraged to become ourselves. God offers us forgiveness and redemption. God offers us all the resources of God's persuasive love. This action is not coercion, for no one can force others to be themselves. We can only nurture their self-creation through our love for them. And this is just what God does for us. God offers us our minds, our emotions, our ability to relate to others, all the characteristics that make us human. All of these resources are there for us if we can only use them to strive toward wholeness and service rather than burnout.

God, Our Nurturing Parent

Ronda quickly walked back to the kitchen table, took up her pen and legal pad, and wrote under the heading "Ten Things I Like About Myself" the following words:

1. I feel good about the fact that I am alive. I have meaning. I am important. God loves me.

Within ten minutes, Ronda had written nine more. She wrote about her public speaking abilities, her skill with plants, and so on. But it was God's love that made all the rest possible.

Like Ronda, persons caught in the second lie of the Messiah Trap do not have a sense of their own value and worth. They insist that their lives do not count as much as those of others. They feel others have a right to mistreat them. Ronda unnecessarily allowed herself to be emotionally abused in her marriage because she felt this was somehow pleasing to God. But only an abusive parent would delight in the mistreatment of a child.

To trust that God is our Nurturing Parent, to trust in the pure, unbounded love of God is to be empowered. It is to believe that every person makes an infinite difference to God. The entire universe is forever changed by our presence in the world, because God makes our lives everlastingly a part of God's life. The life of every person, no matter how insignificant from a human perspective, is significant because God loves us.

Ronda was beginning to break away from the Messiah Trap by embracing her own lovableness. Ronda realized that she was lovable, in fact, already loved. Learning to value herself as God valued her, Ronda would be less willing to allow Sid to abuse her emotionally. She did not deserve abuse or punishment. She was a valuable creature who deserved support and nurturance.

In her session the next day, Ronda was bubbling with excitement. "I am beginning to see that God loves me just the way I am, with no strings attached! I have always felt embarrassed about saying anything good about myself," Ronda explained, "because I thought that was prideful. You know, that God would be displeased. But now I can see how distorted my thinking was. God loves me! God delights in me! So of course I can say wonderful things about myself. Treating myself like the treasure I am is what truly pleases God!"

Ronda began to discover that God's pure, unbounded love offers a sense of self-worth. She began to believe that in God's love, she mattered *ultimately*, not temporarily. None of God's actions toward her were to cause pain. As a Nurturing Parent, all of God's activity was intended to nurture her growth as a strong and free person.

Does God Love Us?

Psalms and parables are not the only way we learn about God. God's pure, unbounded love became flesh and blood and walked our earth in the person of Jesus of Nazareth. If we want to see the perfect portrait of God the Attentive and Nurturing Parent, we need to look to Jesus. In his life, death, and resurrection, we have the mightiest of all God's mighty acts. When God wants to do the greatest thing God ever did, reestablish a relationship to sinful human beings, God does not exert brute, coercive force. Instead, God embodies the receptivity and activity of redeeming and empowering love.

What does God do about human sin? How does God deal with our rejection of God's gift of life? Does God, like an Absent Parent, simply leave us to our own devices, ignore us, remain silent and uninvolved? Far from it. Does God, like an Abusive Parent, strike out at us in anger over our rejection and punish us or destroy us? Not at all. God, who is pure, unbounded love, accepts our human life so completely as to take on our human nature. God does this not in the person of a great, world-famous king. Instead, when God is born as a human being it is in a tiny, out-of-the-way land, in a shabby, smelly cattle stall. Then, instead of doing battle against his opponents like a Napoleon or even a David, Jesus suffers and dies. God's ultimate act of wisdom and power looks like an act of foolishness and weakness. God dies on a cross made by human hands. But as Paul says in 1 Corinthians 1:25, "The foolishness of God is wiser than human wisdom, and the weakness of God is stronger than human strength."

God's ultimate act is love. God acts by receiving into God's own life the fullness of human misery and brokenness. And in so doing, God redeems humanity. God's love receives us into itself and then sets us free to become ourselves in a new creation. Jesus is the human manifestation of God's pure, unbounded love. It is the love embodied in this Jesus, who is truly our Messiah, that can offer us the possibility of freedom from the Messiah Traps we have created for ourselves.

Does God love us? Absolutely, with a love that frees us from the lies of the Messiah Trap. Instead of imaging God as an Absent Parent (who is irrelevant to our lives) or an Abusive Parent (who certainly is almighty and active, but whose action harms us), we can see God as the one, supreme lover of us all; the one who makes all other lives a part of God's own life, who includes the processes of growth and self-creation of all others within God's own life, who acts in every other life by holding out to each person her or his own highest possibility of self, whose activity provides the space and support for the growth and wholeness of all others.

With God as our Attentive Parent, we are freed from having to play god in other people's lives. We are released from the first lie of the Messiah Trap ("If I don't do it, it won't get done") to become a part of the redemptive process originating in God's love.

With God as our Nurturing Parent, we will no longer value self-demeaning, masochistic activities. We are released from the second lie of the Messiah Trap ("Everyone else's needs take priority over mine"). Our God takes no pleasure in our pain, rather seeks to be with us and to redeem us through the sorrows and sadness. Inflicting further pain upon ourselves offers no joy to God. Rather, we serve a God who attends to us, nurtures us, and loves us. God loves us so much that our very existence makes an ultimate difference in the universe.

Does God love us? Yes, more than we can fathom. Our task is not to scurry around, busy with the self-deluded tasks of the Messiah Trap, grabbing for more control. Nor are we to sacrifice ourselves to the abusive control of another person. Instead, we are to release control and accept the love of God, allowing our lives to be transformed and renewed.

CHAPTER 9

Can You Love Yourself as Your Neighbor?

*Remember not the former things, nor consider the
things of old. Behold, I am doing a new thing; now
it springs forth, do you not perceive it? I will make
a way in the wilderness and rivers in the desert.*
—Isaiah 43:18

*If anyone is in Christ, they are a new creation; the
old has passed away, behold, the new has come.*
—2 Corinthians 5:17

Scripture tells us that the God who is love does new things,
which bring life, wholeness, freedom, and peace. God creates a
new universe where once there was only emptiness. The people of
Israel are brought out of slavery into a new land. God walks the
earth in our human flesh giving new health to the sick, new
strength to the weak, new sight to the blind. Jesus is raised from
the grave to a new and undying life. A new community is gathered
through the wind and fire of God's Spirit. Throughout Scripture
we learn that God's mighty acts are those of the creation of new
life. The task of those of us who seek to follow God is to learn to let
go and open ourselves to the forces of new creation God offers.

Burned-out Christians, addicted to their helping activities, desperately need God to work a new thing in their lives through love.

They need new life, wholeness, freedom, and peace. For those who labor under idolatrous images of God as an Absent or Abusive Parent, the experience of God as pure, unbounded love may open up the possibility of new creation. At the center of this new creation is the ability to love oneself with the same pure, unbounded love God shows to us.

But this may present a difficulty, for many of us have been taught that self-love is sinful. Of course, there *is* a form of selfishness that is sinful. But this selfishness is really a distortion, not a form, of love. It is not really *love* of self, so much as self-sufficiency, self-absorption, self-addiction, self-idolatry. This sinful addiction to self, in which my interests and needs take precedence over all others, is particularly dangerous for us Americans. We live as if our needs, our consumption of material goods, are the only things that matter. In so doing, we endanger the lives of the needy in the rest of the world.

It is difficult, even dangerous, to speak about a proper Christian self-love. Nevertheless, we must do so and in God's love we can do so. If we do not love ourselves properly the pain, isolation, and inevitable self-destruction caused by the Messiah Trap will remain.

A New Image of Self

Jenny was driving her daughter Tanya home from her soccer game. For the past ten minutes, mother and daughter had talked about little else than the way Mr. Johnson had acted at the game. Carrie Johnson was the team's goalie and a friend of Tanya's. Mr. Johnson had spent the entire game roaring instructions and criticism to his daughter from the sideline.

"Is he always like that?" Jenny asked.

"Yup, every game," said Tanya. "Why does he take it so seriously? Carrie's only thirteen. You would think we were professionals or something the way he yells all the time."

"I have never understood parents who put such unrealistic demands on their children," Jenny remarked as she pulled into the driveway. "Poor Carrie is always under pressure to be perfect. It is cruel to treat a child that way—especially your own."

"And you know what, Mom," Tanya said, "the more Mr. Johnson puts Carrie down for her mistakes, the more she makes. She is so nervous when her father is at our games."

As they walked to the front door, Jenny scowled and said, "Someone needs to tell that man to lighten up! If he doesn't he is going to lose his daughter."

Tanya went downstairs to watch television. Jenny began to work on supper. She had to keep it simple because she had agreed to help host a reception at the church that evening for the new choir director. As Jenny hurriedly peeled some carrots, she felt the tension begin to build in the back of her neck and climb toward her head. Then Jenny had a thought that surprised her so much she dropped the peeler and the last carrot to the floor.

"I went on and on with Tanya about how Mr. Johnson mistreats his daughter Carrie," Jenny said to herself. "But that's just how I mistreat myself. It's always push, push, push. Everything has to be perfect. One little error on a brochure and I punish myself with a three-week guilt trip." Jenny sat down with a stunned look on her face. "If Mr. Johnson doesn't really love Carrie, then I guess I have to face the truth that I don't love myself either."

Many of us are like Jenny. We allow destructive behavior and attitudes toward ourselves that we would consider unacceptable if we observed them in other people. It was easy for Jenny to see that Mr. Johnson's behavior was demeaning and destructive. But she had been mistreating herself in just the same way for years, without a word of protest, without even being aware of what she was doing. Because she was caught in the Messiah Trap, Jenny had been unable to love herself as she would want to see friends, family members, even casual acquaintances loved by other people. More importantly, Jenny had been unable to love herself as God loved her. Her challenge and ours is to discover an appropriate self-love. If we can, then Christians caught in the Messiah Trap may catch sight of a new image of themselves and be freed to treat themselves with the gentleness of love.

God is love. God loves each of us. God is the prodigal father of Jesus' parable, whose unconditional love for us is pure, boundless, and everlasting. Those who claim to love God and seek to follow God's will have no business ignoring, despising, or mistreating anything that God loves. We are to love all that God loves. We are to love all that God loves as purely and boundlessly as we can. This means: *we must love ourselves, for we are loved by God.*

A clue to what appropriate love of self might be is suggested by our definition of love. We said that love has two sides: first, we allow another person to make a difference in our life; then, second, because of the difference the other person makes, we act toward the other person so as to help her or him develop more fully as a person. This is also how we ought to treat ourselves in all that we do, in our work as well as in our play.

To love ourselves is to allow our own health and wholeness to make a difference to us. Since God has created and redeemed us for health and wholeness, we cannot be indifferent to or destructive of ourselves. We are called to be vulnerable to ourselves, open to our deepest feelings and interests, and accepting of our own irreplaceable worth. We do this by letting go, relaxing, and letting ourselves be, just as we let go, relax, and let other people be themselves. To allow our own wholeness as persons to make a real difference means to stop treating ourselves the way those caught in the Messiah Trap treat themselves.

Then, second, on the basis of the difference our own wholeness makes, we must act in every appropriate way to nurture ourselves. We must treat ourselves tenderly. To love ourselves is to let go of the unrealistic demands, the isolation, the strenuous efforts at control, the inability to relax. We are free to respond to ourselves with richness and creativity. We must risk caring for ourselves. If we fail to love ourselves in this way, then we will have mistreated a precious person God loves.

Such love of self is grounded in God's love. We can allow our own health and wholeness to make a difference in our lives, and we can act on the basis of the difference it makes because God loves us in just this same receptive and active way. God's love offers us the possibility of being wholly ourselves.

If we love ourselves as God loves us, then our genuine love for self will not be in competition with our love for others and our love for God; it will harmonize with and bring to fruition these loves. God's love for us is the foundation of an appropriate love of self and a new image of self.

You Are Your Own Closest Neighbor

In the days following the soccer game and her sudden realization that she had not been treating herself with love, Jenny did a lot of thinking. She read about God's commandments, especially the love commandment. She was reminded of Jesus' teaching that all of God's commandments can be summarized in the love of God and the love of neighbor. "Love your neighbor" means to act toward others as God has already acted toward us, she read. "Be holy, for I am holy," God says; "Love, for I am love." But for Jenny, this command to love others, to love our neighbor as ourself, had been distorted to mean, "Love your neighbor by avoiding love of self," even, "Love your neighbor at the cost of destroying yourself." She needed to learn that this command to love also applies to our ways of treating ourselves.

While she was in the church library, Jenny picked up a book she had not noticed before, *The Dialogue,* by St. Catherine of Siena (translated by Suzanne Noffke, New York: Paulist Press, 1980). The watercolor portrait of Catherine on the cover attracted Jenny's attention. Catherine's thin, vulnerable face reminded Jenny of her own.

In the introduction to the book, Jenny learned that Catherine was an Italian woman from the town of Siena, who lived some six hundred years ago. Instead of marrying in her early teens (as was the custom), bearing many children (she was herself the twenty-fourth of twenty-five children), and perhaps dying in childbirth, Catherine devoted her life to God in a unique way, one that enabled her to bear a large family of spiritual children over the centuries. She gave herself to prayer, peacemaking, caring for the sick (especially those with the plague), and writing. Her vision of the Christian life was so profound and persuasive that she became known as Saint Catherine and was given the title Doctor of the Church: an authoritative teacher of Christian faith.

As Jenny read Catherine's spiritual classic, *The Dialogue*, she came upon an idea that laid the foundation for an appropriate love of herself. "In the middle of a discussion of Jesus' command that we love our neighbor," Jenny recalled later, "Catherine made the simple, but for me life-changing, comment that each of us is our own closest neighbor. Because this is true, Catherine said, the divine command to love our neighbor applies to our attitudes and behavior toward ourselves. We have a responsibility not only to treat our near and distant neighbors with love, but also that closest neighbor of all, that one person over whom we have some direct influence—ourselves." The Christian caught in the Messiah Trap needs to take it as a command from the God who is pure, unbounded love to show God's love to themselves, to treat themselves with the same affection, gentleness, and care they believe they ought to show to friends, spouses, parents, children, even strangers.

The life of Catherine of Siena, who offers us the liberating truth that we are each our own closest neighbor, stands as a reminder both to the writers and readers of this book. Tragically, Catherine was not always able to live out her own teaching. She did not always treat herself with the love she felt God had for her. Nor was she always able to care for her own physical needs with the same intensity she showed to others who were sick and needy. Catherine's life ended prematurely because of her failure to eat properly. This shows that *writing* or *reading about* the love of God for us is not the same as *trusting in* the love of God for us as the basis of our self-worth. If we are to learn to love ourselves, then we must do more than just read and write.

As we learn to love ourselves as our neighbor, we break the chains of the Messiah Trap. A person breaking free

1. accepts the fact that God loves him or her just as he or she is;
2. takes the time and effort to care for himself or herself;
3. is able to set realistic goals and limits.

1. Accepts the Fact that God Loves Him or Her Just as He or She Is

Jenny returned home from the church library where she had read about St. Catherine. It was Monday, and she had to finish preparations for the Bible study she would lead the following evening. For the first time in years, Jenny was filled with expectancy and excitement, not frustration and dread.

As her friends filled the living room on a cool Tuesday evening, Jenny could hardly contain her excitement. The study group had been working its way through the Gospel of Luke. The passage for that week was the parable of the Good Samaritan. Her prayerful study of this parable helped to deepen Jenny's understanding of what it might mean for her to love herself as God loved her. She couldn't wait to share her discovery with the other members of the Bible study.

"I know you have all read the parable yourselves at home," Jenny said to the group, "but these words made such an impact on me, I would like to read them out loud." Jenny picked up her Bible, which was open to Luke 10:25–37, and read:

> On one occasion an expert in the law stood up to test Jesus. "Teacher," he asked, "what must I do to inherit eternal life?"
>
> "What is written in the Law?" Jesus replied. "How do you read it?"

He answered, " 'Love the Lord your God with all your heart and with all your soul and with all your strength and with all your mind;' and 'Love your neighbor as yourself.' "

"You have answered correctly," Jesus replied. "Do this and you will live."

But the man wanted to justify himself, so he asked Jesus, "And who is my neighbor?"

In reply Jesus said: "A man was going down from Jerusalem to Jericho, when he fell into the hands of robbers. They stripped him of his clothes, beat him and went away, leaving him half dead. A priest happened to be going down the same road, and when he saw the man, he passed by on the other side. So too, a Levite, when he came to the place and saw him, passed by on the other side. But a Samaritan, as he traveled, came where the man was; and when he saw him, he took pity on him. He went to him and bandaged his wounds, pouring on oil and wine. Then he put the man on his own donkey, took him to an inn and took care of him. The next day he took out two silver coins and gave them to the innkeeper. 'Look after him,' he said, 'and when I return, I will reimburse you for any extra expense you may have.'

"Which of these three do you think was a neighbor to the man who fell into the hands of robbers?"

The expert in the law replied, "The one who had mercy on him."

Jesus told him, "Go and do likewise" (NIV).

With a broad smile on her face, Jenny began to tell the group about her new insight into this parable. "We all know that Jesus uses the parable of the Good Samaritan to show what love of neighbor means. What God has shown me recently is that each of us is our own closest neighbor. If this is true, then we are to love ourselves. We are to treat ourselves as the Good Samaritan treated the injured man in the parable.

"I really needed to hear that message," Jenny continued. "For too long I treated myself the way the priest and the Levite treated the injured man. I passed by my bruised, burned-out self on the other side. I ignored my frantic, unhealthy pace. We should not pass by our own desperate hurt unconcerned. We must recognize our pain. Then we have to find a place of safety and rest where we can begin to have a healing balm applied to our wounded selves. We must be as generous as the Good Samaritan in finding resources for our own healing."

As Jenny learned to love herself as God loved her, she began to reverse the destructive patterns into which the Messiah Trap had led her. As she learned to treat herself as her own closest neighbor, Jenny began to adopt a new lifestyle, the Spiral of Service. Instead of being caught in a cycle of burnout, she found herself growing stronger and fuller as she loved herself and reached out to those around her in loving service.

2. Takes the Time and Effort to Care for Himself or Herself

After some difficulty, Jenny located Kit's phone number. Even though Jenny had deeply missed Kit's support and infectious sense of humor, it had been months since Jenny had made time to do things with her friend. Jenny was thrilled to hear Kit's hello on the phone and to make a luncheon date for later in the week.

When caught in the Messiah Trap, we never seem to have time for ourselves. We have plenty of time for those who need us. But we feel selfish when we need support from others. We are reluctant to draw close to those who have that special knack of helping us sort through difficult issues. We deprive ourselves of those who can make us feel safe by the warmth of their voice. How often do we turn to those who can always get us to giggle no matter how bad it may seem? Because we are so busy trying to earn our worth, we Messiahs never let anyone make a difference in our lives.

Jenny explained to Kit over lunch, "I have been so busy taking care of everyone in my life that I've had no time for taking care of myself. As I realized God really loved me and wanted what was best for me, I began to see that my needs were important too. So," she smiled at her longtime friend, "I asked myself, Who would I most like to spend time with this week? And your name popped into my mind. We used to have such great times together!"

Kit responded carefully, "You know, at first, when you became a Christian, I was happy for you. You seemed to have such joy that I started thinking about God. But then you changed for the worse. Every time I saw you, you were exhausted and irritable. For a while, I kept calling you, but you always were too busy for me. So I finally gave up, on you and on God."

Jenny's eyes grew sad. "Oh, Kit, don't blame God for my addiction. I got off-track by falling into the Messiah Trap. I became confused and went in the wrong direction. I really hope you will give me, and God, a second chance. God loves both of us."

Kit smiled, "Well, I have missed you so much. It really is great to have you back!"

Jenny learned that God was not honored by her addictive helping. In fact, people were hurt and put off by the Messiah Trap. But when she accepted that God loved her, Jenny was free to love herself and others in a truly redeeming way. She experienced a sense of empowerment and self-worth that she passed on to others.

"I was so miserable," Jenny continued, "when I was trying to live for everyone else. I just couldn't take it anymore." Tears welled in her eyes, "I have missed laughing with you and going shopping with you. Just being with you makes my life better."

Kit asked, "Then why did you push me away?"

Jenny explained, "Because I didn't think that my liking to be with you was reason enough to see you. It sounds so odd, to say that out loud. But I felt so obligated to take care of everyone else I felt guilty when I would see or do anything merely because I needed it."

Patting her friend on the hand, Kit smiled, "Well, I'm glad those days are over. You are one of the most special people in the world, as far as I am concerned. You don't have to prove you are good enough to me. I like you just the way you are."

Jenny laughed, "I knew there was a reason why I liked you. You have such good taste!"

Jenny was learning that her needs were important—period. No longer was she being seduced by the second lie of the Messiah Trap, "Everyone else's needs take priority over mine." God's love for Jenny gave her the strength and the permission to spend time caring for herself.

3. Is Able to Set Realistic Goals and Limits

As the Easter pageant drew closer, Jenny once again worked on the brochure. She smiled to herself about the fuss she had made last year over her typographical error. While she was trying her best, she knew that it was impossible to please everyone in the pageant. This year she wasn't working for perfection. Rather, she was enjoying the opportunity to participate in spreading the news that Jesus was alive to love us all.

Jenny had made quite a few changes in her life, all of which could be traced back to the day when she discovered that, because God loved her, she could love herself as her closest neighbor. The changes had certainly not occurred overnight. But Jenny began to believe that God loved her just as she was, with no additional work needed on her part. The more she accepted God's love for her, the less she needed to prove herself. She no longer felt she had to earn God's love by taking on an endless list of activities.

The Messiah Trap creates the illusion that we are on probation, convicted criminals walking a thin line between freedom and prison. We dare not make a mistake. We cannot disappoint anyone or else God will turn away from us and send us back to a dark, cold cell. To be loving, according to the Messiah Trap, is never, ever to say no.

As Jenny learned to love herself, she made a list of all of her activities, and then beside each one she wrote down her motivation for participating. To her surprise, most of her activities were motivated out of obligation, guilt, or pressure from others. In spite of the criticism she received from various church members and friends, Jenny resigned every activity that wasn't rooted in a truly loving motivation. She was learning to allow her actions to be determined by a sense of her own worth and talent rather than by the expectations of others.

As Jenny reviewed her list, she found that she genuinely enjoyed two of her activities: leading the Bible study group and working on the Easter pageant brochure. In these two areas she had been able to express the receptive and active nature of love. She opened herself up to the Bible study members and was able to contribute to their lives as well. Through the brochure, she felt free to express just how much of a difference God was making in her life. Now that she was no longer overextended and exhausted all the time, she had adequate time to prepare, to ponder and pray about her involvement in the Bible study and the design of the brochure. The obligation she used to feel about these activities was replaced by a warm sense of joy.

The love of God gave Jenny the ability to love herself, in fact, to become a new self. She was freed from the first lie of the Messiah Trap, "If I don't do it, it won't get done." Jenny continued to lead her Bible study, not because it wouldn't get done if she didn't do it, but because of the sense of her own worth God's love had given her. Since she no longer felt obligated to work on the brochure, Jenny found that she actually wanted to work on the project. She was convinced that God loved her for who she was, not for what she did. And yet, in God's love, all that she did was offered as a gift of gratitude for God's love.

God's love can release us from the illusion that the whole world depends on us and our actions. It can release us from slavery to our work, especially our work for good. We are free to treat ourselves gently, lovingly, because we no longer have to feel responsible for the new creation that only God can accomplish. And yet we can rest assured that all our acts, however hidden, are never lost but become a part of God.

Jenny was learning to say no—no to her perfectionism, to unrealistic performance demands, to her overextended schedule. As she was free to set realistic goals for herself, she was also finding a new opportunity to say yes—yes to loving herself, to her own creativity, to a balanced, loving lifestyle. Her enthusiasm acted as a magnet that drew people to her.

The previous year, bound by her attempts to make everyone happy, the brochure design was stiff and lifeless. This year's design came straight out of Jenny's gratitude for God. Everyone who saw her sketches commented on the new style. Even the printer, who had never been to church, asked about attending the pageant after seeing her brochure. There was new life in Jenny once she broke free of the Messiah Trap.

When we treat ourselves tenderly and do not make unrealistic demands on ourselves, we naturally become more richly and fully ourselves. The creativity that God has given to each of us can find no expression within the confines of the Messiah Trap. But as we take the risk of loving ourselves as our neighbors, we will be set free to create a life of love for ourselves and everyone we meet.

CHAPTER 10

Can the Church Be a Community of Love?

A new commandment I give you: love one another.
As I have loved you, so you must love one another.
If you have love for one another, then all will know
that you are my disciples.
—John 13:34–35 (TEV)

"Would you be interested in going bowling with me and some of my friends from the women's support group at my church?" Anna asked while munching a sandwich. Maria and Anna were becoming close friends during their lunch breaks at the office.

Smiling with her mouth, but not her eyes, Maria replied, "Oh, thanks for asking, but I'm not very good at bowling."

Anna asked, "Is that the real reason you don't want to go?"

Sighing heavily, Maria replied, "No. To be honest with you, I had a really bad experience with the church a while back and I don't want anything more to do with it. I got no support, only guilt and obligation. I just burned out on all that church stuff."

"Not every church is the same, Maria," Anna pushed. "I really think you'd enjoy these people."

"No, thanks. I don't want to be rude, but I really don't want to go," Maria said.

Anna smiled, "Give me a break, it's just bowling! What do you think we could do to you at the bowling alley?"

Maria burst into a laugh. "Well, I guess I'd be pretty safe in a public place! All right, I'll go. But let me meet you there so I can leave if I get uncomfortable."

Anna smiled, "That's a deal."

What Is the Church?

What is the key identifying mark of the church? Trees can be identified by shape, bark, leaves, and fruit; birds by plumage, voice, habitat, and behavior. What sets the church apart from all other human groups? Buildings? Programs? Organizational structure? Ritual? Lifestyle? Doctrine?

The writers of the New Testament recognize none of these as the key identifying mark of the church. Instead, they point to the quality of relationships between the followers of Christ. Love is the one characteristic that identifies the church. The lines in the chorus that became popular in the late sixties and early seventies are an accurate statement of the New Testament view: "And they'll know we are Christians by our love, by our love; and they'll know we are Christians by our love."

In Matthew 25, Jesus points to love, not doctrine or program, as the measuring stick of our relationship to God:

> "I was hungry and you fed me, thirsty and you gave me drink; I was a stranger and you received me in your homes, naked and you clothed me; I was sick and you took care of me, in prison and you visited me." The righteous will then answer him: "When, Lord, did we ever see you hungry and feed you, or thirsty and give you drink? When did we ever see you a stranger and welcome you into our homes, or naked and clothe you? When did we ever see you sick or in prison, and visit you?" Then the King will answer back, "I tell you, indeed, whenever you did this for one of the poorest brothers and sisters of mine, you did it for me!" (Matthew 25:35–40, TEV).

When Paul is forced to deal with the divisive question of whether Christians could eat meat ritually dedicated to pagan gods, he is convinced that the crucial issue is not theological or ethical. What is crucial is the relationships between Christians who disagree about theological and ethical issues. Since there are no "gods," only one God and one Lord Jesus Christ, it is permissible to eat meat offered to the so-called gods (1 Corinthians 8:4-6). However, Paul refuses to eat meat, even though he knows it to be theologically permissible, because of his love for his fellow believers:

> Such knowledge, however, puffs a person up with pride, but love builds up. . . . Some people are so used to idols that to this very day when they eat such food they still think of it as food that belongs to an idol; their conscience is weak and they feel they are defiled by the food. Food, however, will not bring us any closer to God; we shall not lose anything if we do not eat, nor shall we gain anything if we do eat. Be careful, however, and do not let your freedom of action make those who are weak in the faith fall into sin. . . . And so this weak person, your brother or sister for whom Christ died, will perish because of your knowledge! And in this way you will be sinning against Christ by sinning against your brothers and sisters and wounding their weak consciences. If food makes my brother or sister sin, I myself will never eat meat again, so as not to make my brother or sister fall into sin (1 Corinthians 8:7-9, 11-13, TEV).

The church is meant to be a community of love. Unfortunately, Christ's followers have not always embodied the love of the Christ they follow. The need for a book such as this is created by the destructive and painful reality that some churches have become centers of burnout, not communities of love. There are too many stories of people whose churches have not nurtured freedom and empowerment, release and self-worth. Too often love has been distorted to mean inappropriate self-sacrifice, authoritarianism, domination of others.

121

If Christians are to be fully released from the Messiah Trap, if their churches are to stop setting the Messiah Trap, a new image of the church must be recovered. Just as the new image of the self as our own closest neighbor was based upon the new image of God as pure, unbounded love, so this same love of God provides the foundation for an image of the church as a community of love.

A New Image of the Church

In the Gospel and Letters of John we find the most thorough portrayal of the kind of relationships that ought to exist within the church as a community of love. Chapters 13 through 17 of John's Gospel, the so-called farewell discourse, represent Jesus' last will and testament. In these chapters we find Jesus' final instructions to his followers before the events of Good Friday. Jesus' instructions center around how the community of his followers is to go on after he has been physically taken from them. Jesus promises that he will continue to be present in the community through his Spirit, and he gives the community a new commandment, the commandment to love.

The key clause in this last will and testament is John 15:14–15. Jesus says, "You are my beloved ones, if you do what I command. I do not call you slaves any longer, because a slave does not know what the master is doing. Instead I call you beloved ones, because I told you everything I heard from God" (TEV).

The theme of the reversal of master and slave roles is an important aspect of Jesus' teaching. The masters, those who have been privileged, are judged by Jesus, while the slaves, those who have been deprived, are included and valued. "So the last will be first, and the first last" (Matthew 20:16). "But whoever would be great among you must be your servant, and whoever would be first among you must be slave of all" (Mark 10:43–44). "For everyone who exalts themselves will be humbled, but the ones who humble themselves will be exalted" (Luke 18:14). Jesus' own mission as Messiah is to serve, not be served (Matthew 20:28).

Jesus not only preaches a reversal of master and slave, he also puts it into practice. John 13:1–17 tells how Jesus washes his disciples' feet. In doing this, Jesus is consciously reversing ordinary social roles and relationships. Simon Peter resists at first, because it was unthinkably inappropriate that the master should wash the slave's feet. This scene finds its parallel in the other three Gospels in the account of Peter's confession at Caesarea Philippi (Matthew 16:13–20; Mark 8:27–38; Luke 9:18–27). In response to Jesus' questions, "Who do people say that I am?" and "Who do you say that I am?" Peter responds, "You are the Messiah, the Son of God." But, here too, Jesus does not act and speak as Peter expects the Messiah, his master, to act and speak. Jesus affirms that he is the Messiah, the Son of God, and so, for this very reason, must suffer and be put to death. Peter rebukes Jesus' interpretation of messiahship. Jesus' response is devastating: "Get behind me, Satan" (Mark 8:33).

Only in John 15 does the full significance of Jesus' words and actions concerning the reversal of masters and slaves appear. Jesus refuses any longer to call his followers slaves. Jesus gives them a new name, one that indicates a very different kind of relationship than that of master and slave. Jesus calls his disciples beloved ones. The word is *philoi*, which is usually translated "friends," although it also has a stronger meaning: "lovers" or "beloved ones."

John 15:14–15 shows that the ultimate purpose behind the reversal of master and slave roles is not simply to replace one set of masters with another. Jesus' teaching and practice is aimed at the elimination of all master-slave relationships. Master and slave is no longer an appropriate model for the Christian's relationship to God or to fellow Christians. Instead, we are to relate to one another as beloved ones because, in Jesus Christ, God relates to us as beloved ones.

We believe that all relationships within the church are to be thought of as relationships between beloved ones. All relationships: ministry staff to each other; ministers to lay persons; board members to lay persons; choir members to each other; even two people sitting next to one another in the pew. The church is to be characterized by love, by relationships of trust and mutuality between beloved ones, not by the coercive relationships of domination and submission between master and slave, leader and follower.

Receptivity and Activity
Toward the Beloved One

"Well?" Anna asked anxiously.

"Well," Maria smiled reluctantly, "I actually had a good time with your friends."

"Great!" Anna exclaimed. "See, we're not all out to get you." Maria replied, "It is a surprise to me, but the people I met in your group were really nice and supportive. You know, they actually seemed interested in me. In me!"

Anna's friends had approached Maria with open hearts. They shared their stories. They listened attentively when Maria told about herself. She described a new software package she was using on the computer at the office. One of the women, Fran, was so excited by Maria's description that she said she was going to encourage her supervisor to order the same program. Maria said, "It was so wonderful to be accepted, to be treated like I had something to offer."

Anna asked, "Are you interested in coming with me to our monthly prayer meeting?"

Maria paused. "Getting any more involved scares me a little. But I had such a good time the other night. I felt valued and supported. OK, I'll give it a try."

What does it mean to treat other persons as beloved ones? How do we live out Jesus' command to love one another, to love our neighbor as ourself?

Recall, once again, the definition of love suggested earlier. To love is to allow another person to make a real difference in one's life, and, because of the difference the other person makes, to act toward the other person so as to assist her or him to develop more fully as a person. This view of love can transform all our relationships, including relationships within the church. Of course, we do not relate to every person with the same intensity or the same level of intimacy. But whether we are talking about our relationships to spouses, children, parents, friends, co-workers, even strangers, we are to love them in this sense.

First, love means accepting another person unconditionally for who they are. To love is to care for someone in such a way that nothing they do or fail to do can change our acceptance of them. Anna's friends illustrated their blossoming love for Maria by allowing her to make a difference in their own lives. They received her knowledge of computer programs as a gift. Maria was not treated like a poor, helpless woman who was too inept to get along by herself. She was accepted and allowed to make a difference, with no strings attached.

This involves risk, the risk of opening ourselves to others as real people, not trying to make them into extensions of ourselves. When caught in the Messiah Trap, we tend to think of love as the possession or ownership of another person rather than the acceptance of them for who they are. Too often love is conditional: "I will love you, if . . ." Genuine love, on the other hand, involves letting go of our control over other persons.

Second, because the other person, the beloved one, makes such a difference to us, we act toward them so that everything we do is aimed at helping them grow. They are valuable for who they are, not because of what they can do for us. Because the group recognized Maria to be a valuable person, one who contributed to their lives, they responded by offering the support and friendship she needed. Everyone's life was enriched.

This also involves risk, the risk of exerting ourselves for another person, of working hard for their wholeness. There are times to protect, defend, nurture, confront, and support those we love. But our actions, however helpful, cannot take the place of that person, the beloved one. We Messiahs mistakenly try to live their lives for them. Nothing could be further from the truth.

To love is to give space for the other person to grow and act and be. But this is not empty space. It is, rather, free space with a solid foundation underneath. Our acts cannot coerce or make the beloved one do something. That would be a return to the master-slave relationship, not the relationship between beloved ones.

The actions of love are something like those of raising tender young plants. The tiny seedlings need our support. We have to work, to exert ourselves, in order to put them in a sunny place, to water them, to fertilize them, eventually to transplant them and stake them up. But in doing this we are only aiding the growth process of the plant itself. We are not doing the growing for the plant. And if we fuss too much with the young plant, if we were to pull it up to see how the roots are developing, we would kill the plant.

So, too, with the beloved one. We can offer our resources. We can, and should, make gifts of ourselves for the beloved one. It is appropriate to offer time, energy, talent, to support and enrich their lives. But we cannot impose ourselves on the beloved one or we will smother their growth. We cannot, like the codependents, clutch their lives too tightly or we will rip up the beloved one, roots and all.

This dual risk of love is suggested in the most famous description of love in the entire Bible, 1 Corinthians 13. Paul writes,

> Love is patient and kind; love is not jealous or boastful; it is not arrogant or rude. Love does not insist on its own way; it is not irritable or resentful; it does not rejoice at wrong, but rejoices in the right. Love bears all things, believes all things, hopes all things, endures all things (verses 4–7).

Each person within the church, ourselves included, needs both to be treated with such love and to treat others in this way. We are called to risk opening ourselves to others. We also need to find others who accept us unconditionally and support and nurture us as we grow.

Many Members, One Spirit of Love

Maria was a bit apprehensive the night she went to the prayer meeting with Anna. She was afraid the loving experience wouldn't last. While Maria enjoyed the Scripture reading and discussion, she was expecting everyone to act as if they had no problems. As she told Anna on the ride over, "Everyone in my old church pretended to be perfect. No one was ever honest about their struggles." Maria was also waiting for the "big sell," the announcements of all the work that needed to be done and the pressure for people to volunteer. But the big sell never came.

Instead, Maria found herself listening to people talk about their genuine problems, problems in their marriages, jobs, health. No one pretended to be better than anyone else. The group members also shared the joys of their successes and accomplishments. "Hmm," Maria thought to herself, "no one seems to be putting on false humility here."

One of the women talked about how painful her divorce had been. Maria surprised herself by talking about the abuse her husband had heaped on her and the children. When she finished, Maria was sure the group would just sit in stunned silence, judging her for leaving her husband.

Nothing of the sort happened. The woman sitting next to Maria put her arms around her and held her tightly. A number of the other group members were in tears at Maria's story. No one seemed to avoid Maria that night or in the months to come, as Maria began to attend the church regularly. Everyone seemed to say, "We love you, Maria, no matter what. We realize your marriage was horrible. We support your decision to protect yourself and your children and move back here."

Not only did the people of Maria's new church really listen to her pain without judging her, they were also wonderful at actively supporting her. Fran agreed to drive Maria's son and daughter from the school to the YMCA after-school program. This meant

Maria no longer had to work odd hours. The pastor of the church put Maria into contact with the city's housing office to see if a safer, more appropriate apartment could be found for Maria and the children. And Anna promised to go with Maria every week to an aerobics class to help Maria get down to a more healthy weight. The church made Maria feel valuable and supported.

Within this community of love Maria discovered a place to offer her own talents. A whiz at computers, Maria was asked to consult with the church board as they tried to decide which computer system to install. She helped select the appropriate software for the system and then trained the paid staff on the new programs. No longer feeling alone and overextended, Maria found a community that loved her enough to allow her to contribute herself, a community that enhanced her self-esteem through their support.

Within a community of love, such as Maria experienced, we can serve and survive. We can serve our beloved ones without burnout, without falling into the Messiah Trap. The reason is that in a community of beloved ones, the intrinsic value of both the one who serves and the one who is served is recognized and protected. No longer is the one served looked upon as a victim. No longer is the one who serves a Messiah. Both are gently supported as persons who are the beloved ones of God.

Paul's image of the church as the body of Christ fits such a community of love perfectly (1 Corinthians 12:12-31). The church, Paul writes, is one body with many members. Because the life of the body is a gift of the one Spirit of God's love, there need be no division. The eye cannot say to the hand, "I don't need you," or, "I need you only as the poor victim I must rescue." If any beloved one in the community suffers, all suffer; if one rejoices, all rejoice. Each person is a beloved one who makes a difference to the others. Each person acts toward all other beloved ones to help them grow. No longer is the body divided among masters and slaves, the victims to be helped and the Messiahs who are burned out helping.

CHAPTER 11

Can You Live on the Spiral of Service?

What then shall we say to this? If God is for us, who is against us? For I am certain that neither death, nor life, nor angels, nor principalities, nor things present, nor things to come, nor powers, nor height, nor depth, nor anything else in all creation, will be able to separate us from the love of God in Christ Jesus our Lord.
—Romans 8:31, 38–39

"Are you sure you want to volunteer for the ministry to the homeless?" Ted, the program's coordinator, asked cautiously. "It's not that we don't need volunteers," he paused, feeling uncomfortable, "but I didn't get the impression you had a very good experience when you volunteered before."

Charles's face broke into a wide grin. "You are right about that, Ted. I was involved in this ministry for all the wrong reasons back then. But things have changed for me now. I'm here for different reasons, and I was hoping you could give me a second chance."

Ted shook Charles's hand with a glint in his eye. "Well, you sound like you've thought this through. You are certainly welcome to the ministry team." A thrill of excitement came over Charles as he walked toward the kitchen. "If this experience is anything like Argentina," he thought to himself, "I'm in for a lot of learning and a lot of love."

Plenty, Not Scarcity

When caught in the Messiah Trap, we operate from the perspective of scarcity. We assume that there is not enough to go around: not enough love, not enough self-worth, not enough strength, not enough support. So, out of neediness and want, emptiness and lack, we Messiahs give what little we have and end up with nothing. Our self-sacrifice, since it is not an expression of love but of obligation and manipulation, does not result in healing and growth. Our lives are damaged, even destroyed, and those we try to help do not genuinely benefit. The Messiah Trap, with its lie of scarcity, leads to death.

The good news of God's love is that there is plenty: plenty of love, self-worth, strength, support. God's pure love knows no bounds. When we love ourselves and others as God loves us, we can learn how to be of genuine service to those around us. When we love as God loves, we can give out of a sense of plenty.

Perhaps the classic New Testament passage about service is Philippians 2:5–11, which begins: "Your attitude ought to be the same as that of Christ Jesus: who, being in very nature God, did not consider equality with God something to be grasped, but made himself nothing, taking the very nature of a servant, being made in human likeness" (verses 5–7, NIV). This is true service. But notice that Jesus Christ's service was rooted in abundance, not scarcity; in love, not in the lies of the Messiah Trap. Why? Because in Christ one finds the very nature of God, the fullness of God dwelling in bodily form. It is out of the abundance of God, an abundance that is uncontainable, that our Lord offers himself in service to others. Out of the fullness of love, not out of the emptiness of need, God made and redeemed the world through Jesus Christ.

Escaping the Messiah Trap

As we acknowledge that there is abundance in God, we must also recognize our own human limitations. The Messiah Trap promotes the lie "If I don't do it, it won't get done." When caught in this lie, we take on an exaggerated, unrealistic sense of responsibility. The Spiral of Service, however, asks the question, "What is my unique contribution?"

Ponder for a moment the fact that there has never been another human being like you. You are unique with your own special configuration of talents, insights, capacity for intimacy and creativity. The Spiral of Service offers you a place to celebrate and share your uniqueness. No longer sidetracked by the obligation, you are free to develop your unique self. No longer attempting the impossible, you are free to contribute yourself as directed by love. In the Spiral of Service, the task is not to act as if you were God, as if you were infinite. Rather, you are free to let God be the source of abundance while you contribute your finite, but important, part.

"I used to feel like I was earning God's approval when I did something for somebody else," Charles explained to the homeless ministry team at their first meeting. "But now I realize that I am already loved. I don't have to be here today. I could be home doing a number of other things and God would still love me. But I chose to return to this ministry because I have something to contribute. There are a number of talents I want to share with those who will participate in our ministry, both the team members and the homeless. I'm here because I want to be here!" Charles had begun to travel down the path of plenty, the path of love. While he knew that it was not an easy path, he was convinced it was one built on God's abundance.

A second lie promoted by the Messiah Trap is "Everyone else's needs take priority over mine." Wearing down our self-esteem, this lie binds us to a self-destructive pattern of never saying no. The Spiral of Service points to a life of balance where everyone, *including ourselves*, gets a turn.

At that first meeting, Charles faced the challenge of following the Spiral of Service or becoming ensnared in the Messiah Trap. As the team worked out the schedule for its various programs, it quickly became clear they had fewer volunteers than were needed.

As the group discussed the problem, the pressure for each member to volunteer additional time began to build. Charles shifted anxiously in his seat and then spoke out. "I think it is very important that we not feel pressured to give more than we are able."

"But what about the street people?" Ted asked. "What are you suggesting, that we just close up because we don't want to be inconvenienced? What do I tell those people who come to the door asking for food: 'Sorry, no one here cares about you'?"

Genuinely annoyed, Charles responded, "Ted, we are all here because we do care. I care, but I am not God. Feeding the homeless is not my responsibility alone, and, in fact, it is not the responsibility of this church alone. I am here to do my part with God as my source of strength. Getting caught up in some false sense of self-importance does not seem helpful to me."

Ted responded, "Charles, I'm not trying to sound grandiose. I am just asking how we are going to cover the hours scheduled for the meals program."

Charles nodded, understanding Ted's concern. "It seems to me we have a couple of options. We can recruit more volunteers or we can limit the number of meals we can provide this fall. But pushing the team members to become overextended and burned out cannot be what God wants for us."

Charles, Ted, and the ministry team were struggling with a very common dilemma for those who work in human services. There always seem to be more needs than resources, more questions than answers, more tears than comfort. But Charles, dedicated to the Spiral of Service, was not seduced by the lies of the Messiah Trap. He recognized that he was utterly dependent upon God. Knowing that God is the source of abundance, Charles avoided the temptation to take that responsibility upon himself. "I'm not going to play god in these people's lives," Charles told the group. "We must honor God by trusting in God's abundance. We are to give what portion we can." Charles was learning that we do not show our love for God by overextending ourselves. We are called to accept ourselves as we truly are, with our limitations as well as with the gifts we have to share.

Charles had begun to reverse the characteristics of the person caught in the Messiah Trap. Like Charles, a person living on the Spiral of Service is one who

1. relates to others with the receptivity and activity of love;
2. is able to establish, protect, and nurture peer and intimate relationships;
3. is able to belong to the group and retain a sense of self;
4. takes satisfaction in a job well done;
5. is able to problem-solve effectively.

1. Relates to Others with the Receptivity and Activity of Love

Charles was busy serving meals when up walked Sam. With chagrin, Charles remembered how verbally abusive he had been to Sam when he had found Sam's bottle collection on top of his car. He also realized that he had never apologized for his actions. Sam coldly took the tray from Charles's hands but would not return the smile. After everyone had been served, Charles sat down by Sam and told him how sorry he was for his actions.

When we are caught in the Messiah Trap, we look down on the people we help. We pretend that they need us for their survival. When we try to earn our worth by helping others, we use them to bolster our sagging self-esteem. Without meaning to, we convey to others the message "You are inferior because you need me, and I am superior because I can help you."

As Charles threw off the chains of the Messiah Trap, he was able to view others in a new light. Sam was no longer an inferior person Charles so kindly stooped to aid. Sam became a human being of infinite worth, someone who deserved to be treated with respect and concern. At the next team meeting Charles said, "I realized that I hadn't apologized to Sam because I didn't really view him as a human being. Now that my attitude has changed, it is fun to spend time with him. We sit together nearly every meal I serve." Charles began to laugh. "That guy is so funny! I never knew he had a sense of humor! It doesn't matter how I feel when I get there, Sam can get me laughing in no time at all. I always feel better after I've seen him."

Charles was experiencing the receptive side of love. Caught in the Messiah Trap, we tell ourselves that we show our love for others by how much we do to help them. In the Spiral of Service, love is first illustrated by how much we allow others to affect us. As Charles began to treat Sam like a human being, he was able to see, for the first time, the gifts and treasures in this man. Charles was able to receive Sam's gift of humor. The moment Charles allowed Sam to make a difference in Charles's life was the moment Charles really began to love Sam.

The second side of love, that of contributing in a truly nurturing way, was now open to Charles. Before, Charles saw his contribution as the food he served, the time he donated, the great sacrifice of energy he made. But these were false contributions seen from the perspective of the Messiah Trap.

Ted asked the group, "Have the rest of you noticed a difference in Sam?" When the group said they had, Ted continued, "Sam seems to have come alive since Charles returned to the ministry. What are you doing for him?"

Charles shrugged, "Nothing. I haven't been doing anything special. I just laugh at his jokes!" Charles, without knowing it, was giving Sam the most valuable of gifts: respect. By enjoying Sam's sense of humor, Charles communicated loud and clear that Sam was a valued person. Sam had something he could be proud of, a special gift that was received in love. Charles may have provided Sam with food he needed, but, even more, Sam received a place of honor in Charles's life.

2. Is Able to Establish, Protect, and Nurture Peer and Intimate Relationships

Charles hung up the phone perplexed. The shelter had just called him at work saying they needed emergency coverage. However, Charles had promised to take his daughter to dinner for their special night out. He felt pressured to say yes to the request from the shelter. He thought to himself, "How can I tell them I think it's more important that I take my daughter out to dinner than feed the hungry?" He stopped and realized that while he valued his ministry, it was his daughter's turn for his attention. He called the shelter back and told them they would have to find someone else.

When we're caught in the Messiah Trap, the people in our personal lives always get shortchanged. Our spouses, children, parents, and friends are last on the Messiah's list. If we are involved in activities that foster the lies of the Messiah Trap, we will find that others expect us to put our personal lives on the back burner. It is not uncommon for Christians who are addictively helping others, either vocationally or as volunteers, to neglect their own families and friends. This neglect is often justified as devotion to God.

The Spiral of Service, in contrast, is a life of balance, where everyone gets a turn, even those in our personal life. When we are loving in a balanced way, receptively and actively, we have time for developing friendships that last. Since we value our children, we make time for their concerns. Our spouses become more than obligations or appendages to our work. We become interested in seeing their gifts and talents developed.

Charles had seen how important his family was to him in Argentina. Back in the States, with the pressures to perform, he found it difficult at times to keep his priorities straight. When he pulled up to the house to pick up his daughter, she came running out to the car with a worried look on her face. "Are we still going out?" she asked with fear in her eyes. "The shelter called here and said they needed you down there. I told them you were still at work. Do you have to go?"

Charles knew at that moment he had made the right choice. "No, darling. This is your night. I love you and don't need to be anyplace in the world but here with you."

"Oh, Daddy!" She threw her arms around his neck. "I love you so much!"

3. Is Able to Belong to the Group and Retain a Sense of Self

Charles looked worriedly at his watch as the team meeting dragged an hour past the scheduled adjournment time. He had so enjoyed the support he received from the other members and felt uneasy about cutting them off. But this was the third meeting in a row that had run over, and Charles was uncomfortable with this pattern. After summoning his courage, he spoke up and asked that the meetings be structured so that business could be taken care of in the allotted time. He received a few icy stares, but the knot in his stomach started to relax.

Charles, once a "lone ranger," had begun to enjoy the team meetings. He confided to the group, "I used to dread these meetings as just another obligation. I never got anything out of them because I would never let anyone know I needed any encouragement or feedback. Not me!" Charles pounded his chest. "I was Super Christian!"

A sense of isolation often haunts those of us caught in the Messiah Trap. We are so busy trying to feel special that we often end up feeling different, even odd. Perched on our pedestals, we do not dare show our own weaknesses for fear of being considered inept or damaged goods. So we pretend to be together, with no problems and, sadly, with no close friends.

But when we live on the Spiral of Service, we are free to receive support and nurturance from those around us. We do not have to pretend we are perfect in order to feel loved. On the contrary, we realize that the first step in love is to accept others unconditionally and to be accepted by others. When that happens, we can relax and be ourselves, flaws and all.

While we become more able to receive the acceptance and nurturance of others, we can also become less dependent upon other people's approval for our sense of self. When caught in the Messiah Trap, we are desperate for approval. We help and help and help, all in the hope that someone will tell us we are special, we are needed, we are important. As we live on the Spiral of Service, we are grounded in God's love for us. We can receive legitimate support and encouragement from others, without any longer needing their approval to validate our self-worth.

After Charles had expressed his feelings about the length of the meetings, he sat quietly, hoping that Ted would bring things to a close. Instead, Ted announced there were still a couple of very important items that needed to be discussed. Before Ted could continue, Charles said calmly, "I am sorry, but I have to leave now. We are already an hour overtime. I'll be glad to contribute to this discussion next week." In silence, the group watched Charles walk out of the room.

In the past, Charles would have sat and endured the meeting, his stomach twisted in knots with resentment. So fearful that the others might think poorly of him, Charles would do anything to please the group. Now, while Charles did not want to be rude or inappropriate, he also was unwilling to be manipulated by the group's opinion. He explained to Sara that evening, "I feel very good about how I handled myself today. I was kind but firm. I love those people, but there are times I must set some limits for myself."

4. Takes Satisfaction in a Job Well Done

Several weeks later, Charles showed up at the team meeting with a huge cake. When asked what it was for, he proudly explained that, since the beginning of the fall, the ministry had provided meals to over five hundred different people! Cutting a big slice Charles announced, "It's time to celebrate!"

There are no celebrations for those caught in the Messiah Trap. There is no time for parties, for laughter, for play. Life is restricted to its trials and pain. Because of the perspective of scarcity, time taken up with parties is considered to be time wasted. Celebrations are considered frivolous, perhaps even immoral.

For those on the Spiral of Service, however, play is an integral part of living. Celebration and laughter are necessary ingredients to our nourishment. Because we live life out of abundance, not scarcity, we are free to take time to congratulate ourselves on a job well done. Rejoicing together, we can enjoy the music, food, entertainment, and companionship for which God has created us.

Time spent in play is time well spent. Only in the Messiah Trap do we find ourselves enemies of joy and play and laughter. Our lives and our world are surrounded by God's love. We are free to receive love, give love, and celebrate love. Charles, once a reserved man who had no time for frivolity, now found himself interested in having fun! "I know this is a surprise to all of you," Charles said, as the group members stared at him in amazement, "but this is the new me! And I say it's time to reward ourselves for all the hard work we've put in."

Ted laughed, picking up a piece of cake, "Well, I don't think you'll hear much complaining from us. Let's celebrate!"

5. Is Able to Problem-Solve Effectively

The winter was especially severe and brought more people to the shelter than had been anticipated. Desperate for food, clothing, and bedding, Ted called an emergency meeting to discuss the problem. The group felt discouraged and overwhelmed. Charles dragged in a blackboard and began to write down all the ideas the group came up with. As the blackboard was filled, the group's morale lifted and several new alternatives were found.

Creativity cannot take root in the soil of scarcity. The horrendous pressures of the Messiah Trap often leave us too exhausted and overwhelmed to come up with new solutions to old problems. Christians caught in the Messiah Trap are convinced that there is not enough to go around. When faced with a genuine crisis, we often assume there are no new answers.

At first, as Charles tried to solicit ideas, the group simply sat in silence. Finally, a woman named Louise said, "Well, maybe all of us could donate more food and blankets." As one caught in the Messiah Trap, Louise was limited in her ability to problem-solve. Living in scarcity, she assumed that if she didn't help these people, no one else would. (First lie: "If I don't do it, it won't get done.") "I just can't stand to think of those poor people going hungry," she sighed. "As long as there is food in my kitchen and there are blankets in my house, I haven't done enough."

Ray, another volunteer, asserted that every team member should double their commitment to the ministry. "How can we go to our warm homes with those people freezing to death out there?" Ray had fallen for the lie "Everyone else's needs take priority over mine." Always pitting his needs against someone else's, Ray assumed that he was being selfish when he cared for his own legitimate needs.

Charles wrote these ideas on the board, but he hoped to generate some alternatives that didn't reflect the lies of the Messiah Trap. Heading the group in a different direction, Charles asked, "How many other churches are there in this community?" The group estimated around thirty churches of various denominations. "How about if we contact these other congregations to recruit volunteers and supplies?"

Allison jumped in, "That's a great idea. And what about where we work? Couldn't we talk to some of our employers and see if they could donate some of the things we need?"

"I've got an idea," Eleanor said. "My daughter started working at a restaurant in town. She told me that at the end of the day they throw out piles of unused bread and other food. Maybe they would let us pick up the leftovers at the end of the day."

Charles smiled to himself as he wrote as fast as he could, trying to keep up with all the ideas. Yes, there is abundance in God's love for us once we break free of the scarcity of the Messiah Trap.

The Spiral of Service

The Messiah Trap ensnares us in a Cycle of Burnout. We become enslaved to a compulsive, codependent way of life that drains us of our energy, resources, and relationships. It is a wild, downward spin that can leave us confused and damaged.

By contrast, the Spiral of Service is based on an accurate understanding of the God who is love; it is motivated by the receptivity and activity of love. We are drawn joyfully into an upward swirl of growth and intimacy. Secure in God's love, we are free to set realistic limits, not obligated to burn out. Relying on God's infinite resources, we no longer have to try to meet every need we see out of our limited supply. In the Spiral of Service, there is enough— enough for everyone, including *you*.

Further Reading

Readers who are interested in the development of the ideas in this book may consult our earlier works:

Berry, Carmen Renee. *When Helping You Is Hurting Me: Escaping the Messiah Trap.* San Francisco: Harper & Row, 1988.

Taylor, Mark Lloyd. *God is Love: A Study in the Theology of Karl Rahner.* Atlanta: Scholars Press, 1986.

In addition, the following books may be helpful:

Beattie, Melody. *Codependent No More.* San Francisco: Harper & Row, 1987.

Fortune, Marie Marshall. *Keeping the Faith: Questions and Answers for the Abused Woman.* San Francisco: Harper & Row, 1987.

Johnson, Robert. *Inner Work.* San Francisco: Harper & Row, 1986.

Kelsey, Morton. *The Other Side of Silence: A Guide to Christian Meditation.* New York: Paulist Press, 1976.

Larsen, Earnie. *Stage II Recovery.* San Francisco: Harper & Row, 1987.

———. *Stage II Relationships.* San Francisco: Harper & Row, 1987.

Narramore, Kathy, and Alice Hill. *Kindred Spirits.* Grand Rapids: Zondervan Publishing House, 1985.

Parham, A. Phillip. *Letting God.* San Francisco: Harper & Row, 1987.

Peck, M. Scott. *The Road Less Traveled.* New York: Simon & Schuster, 1978.

Schaef, Anne Wilson. *Co-Dependence.* San Francisco: Harper & Row, 1987.

Schaeffer, Brenda. *Is It Love or Is It Addiction?* San Francisco: Harper & Row, 1987.

The Twelve Steps of Alcoholics Anonymous. San Francisco: Harper & Row, 1987.

The following articles and books were helpful in the development of a new image of love:

Andolsen, Barbara Hilkert. "*Agape* in Feminist Ethics." *The Journal of Religious Ethics* 9 (1981): 69–83.

D'Arcy, M. C. *The Mind and the Heart of Love.* New York: Henry Holt, 1947.

Farley, Margaret. "New Patterns of Relationship: Beginnings of a Moral Revolution." *Theological Studies* 36 (1975): 627–46.

———. *A Study of the Ethics of Commitment within the Context of Theories of Human Love and Temporality.* Ann Arbor: University Microfilms, 1978.

Hazo, Robert G. *The Idea of Love.* New York: Frederick Praeger, 1967.

Luijpen, William. *Existential Phenomenology.* Translated by Henry Koren. Pittsburgh: Duquesne University Press, 1960.

Nédoncelle, Maurice. *Love and the Person.* Translated by Ruth Adelaid. New York: Sheed and Ward, 1966.

Toner, Jules. *The Experience of Love.* Washington, D.C.: Corpus Books, 1968.

Williams, Daniel Day. *The Spirit and the Forms of Love.* New York: Harper & Row, 1968.

For a more thorough discussion of the image of God sketched in this book, the following sources might be consulted:

Hartshorne, Charles. *The Divine Relativity: A Social Conception of God.* New Haven: Yale University Press, 1948.

Ogden, Schubert. *The Reality of God and Other Essays,* second edition. New York: Harper & Row, 1977.